Why you should read
Your Life...Well Spent

"I have observed that books related to financial principles focus on the current task of managing one's money today. Russ's book *Your Life...Well Spent* takes the LONGER-TERM PERSPECTIVE of looking at plans for a person's career and giving. This book HELPED CHANGE MY LIFE with proper financial and life goals. DON'T MISS IT."

JOEL MANBY, CEO, HERSCHEND FAMILY ENTERTAINMENT

"I have had the privilege of working alongside Russ with multiple families, and I'VE OBSERVED FIRSTHAND THESE PRINCIPLES put into practice. The focus on a HEALTHY GENERATIONAL TRANSFER OF WISDOM is one that will ENRICH YOUR FAMILY and preserve YOUR LEGACY."

DR. RON L. BRAUND, FAMILY BUSINESS TRANSITIONS

"Provides a COMPREHENSIVE LOOK AT MONEY AND YOUR LIFE...a NECESSARY INVESTMENT for anyone who wants to think correctly about how to earn, spend, [and] donate...money."

HOWARD G. HENDRICKS, DISTINGUISHED PROFESSOR EMERITUS,
LEADERSHIP AND CHRISTIAN EDUCATION,
DALLAS THEOLOGICAL SEMINARY

"Without the information in this book, your budget may be balanced but unwise, your bookkeeping may be timely but reflect only temporal values. This is the BOOK TO READ FIRST, before any others, for the RENEWING OF YOUR FINANCIAL MIND."

BRUCE WILKINSON, AUTHOR, *PRAYER OF JABEZ* AND *YOU WERE BORN FOR THIS*

"I appreciate the BIBLICAL MIND-SET backed by PROFESSIONAL EXPERIENCE that goes into Russ's work. Once again Russ has gone BEYOND THE NUTS AND BOLTS to focus the reader's attention on life's big picture."

AUSTIN PRYOR, PUBLISHER, SOUNDMINDINVESTING.COM

"A REMARKABLY WRITTEN REMINDER that the BOTTOM LINE OF LOVING FAMILIES isn't about money, it's a LIFE WELL SPENT."

TIM KIMMEL, AUTHOR, SPEAKER, FAMILY COUNSELOR,
EXECUTIVE DIRECTOR, FAMILY MATTERS

"EYE-OPENING READING about marriage, parenting, training children, balancing life, and financial planning, written like I've never read before. I WAS HOOKED FROM THE FIRST CHAPTER."

GEORGE FOOSHE, FINANCIAL COUNSELOR, AUTHOR

"Ours is a nation of families who are exhausted from haste. But, life *is not* a 100-yard dash, it's a marathon. Pace is more important than haste. RUSS CROSSON offers a PERSPECTIVE OF REMARKABLE CLARITY AND SIMPLICITY that will give your family pace for your race."

STEVE FARRAR, AUTHOR, FOUNDER/CHAIRMAN,
MEN'S LEADERSHIP MINISTRIES

"This book will CHALLENGE YOUR THINKING. It makes a SIGNIFICANT CONTRIBUTION toward understanding the BIBLICAL PERSPECTIVE OF MONEY AND POSSESSIONS. I pray it will stimulate you to become financially faithful."

HOWARD DAYTON, FOUNDER, COMPASS–FINANCES GOD'S WAY

"This book is a MUCH-NEEDED ANTIDOTE to unbiblical thinking regarding finances. Russ Crosson's emphasis on 'posterity' rather than 'prosperity' and eternal rather than temporal investments, if applied, will make you eternally grateful."

WALTER A. HENRICHSEN, AUTHOR

"This book captures KEY BIBLICAL INSIGHTS in the area of our prosperity. And it comes from a man who 'walks the talk.' Russ Crosson meets the challenge of FAIR-MINDEDNESS and READINESS mentioned in Acts 17:11. Here is a book for us to learn from."

GAYLE M. JACKSON, FORMER PRESIDENT,
CAD SYSTEMS, INC., AUTHOR

"Although this book offers a WEALTH OF PRACTICAL FINANCIAL ADVICE, it takes a SIGNIFICANT STEP beyond the 'how tos' of money management to answer the MORE VITAL 'WHY' QUESTIONS. I have seen Russ Crosson consistently model these truths in his own life and have witnessed their impact in the lives of others, including me!"

TIM KALLAM, PASTOR

"Russ Crosson always keeps the big picture in mind when it comes to money. He reminds us to LOOK AT MONEY FROM AN ETERNAL, LIFELONG PERSPECTIVE. That's why this book is a KEY TO YOUR LIFE WELL SPENT."

BRYANT WRIGHT, SR., PASTOR,
JOHNSON FERRY BAPTIST CHURCH,
ATLANTA, GA

"Russ Crosson does an EXCELLENT job of taking us BACK TO THE BASICS, not only of finance, but how to integrate IMPORTANT PRINCIPLES into our total life system."

COLONEL NIMROD MCNAIR, PRESIDENT, MCNAIR ASSOCIATES, INC.

Your Life... Well Spent

RUSS CROSSON

HARVEST HOUSE PUBLISHERS
EUGENE, OREGON

YOUR LIFE...WELL SPENT
Copyright © 1994 by Russ Crosson
Published 2012 by Harvest House Publishers
Eugene, Oregon 97402
www.harvesthousepublishers.com

ISBN 978-0-7369-8210-8 (pbk.)
ISBN 978-0-7369-8211-5 (eBook)

Library of Congress Cataloging-in-Publication Data

Crosson, Russ, 1953-
[Life well spent]
Your life—well spent / Russ Crosson.
    p. cm.
Originally published: A life well spent. Nashville: Thomas Nelson, © 1994.
Includes bibliographical references (p.).
Library of Congress Control Number:2019957916
1. Finance, Personal—Religious aspects—Christianity.   2. Wealth—Religious aspects—Christianity.   3. Christian giving.   4. Families—Religious life I. Title.
HG179.C75 2012
332.024—dc23

                                                        2011021676

To Clark, Reed, and Chad, my posterity,
whom I pray will manifest the truths shared in this book
and pass them on to the generations that
come after them to the glory of God.

Acknowledgments

As with any such undertaking, this book would have been impossible without the assistance and encouragement of countless people. Most importantly, I am grateful to Julie, my wife of 40 years, who is a constant source of encouragement to me. Without her unwavering love, support, and devotion, and her continual training and teaching of our children, the concepts shared in this book would only be hollow words with no substance.

I also owe a debt of gratitude to my partners at Ronald Blue & Co. for allowing me the time to work on this project and from whom many of the insights in this book were gained. Very special thanks go to Chip Vaughan, Curt Knorr, Angie Wells, Barry Vaughan, Bert Harned, and Scott Houser for their detailed reading and comments on the manuscript. Their input, which is contained throughout these pages, was invaluable in developing this final product.

I am also grateful to Bob Hawkins, Terry Glaspey, Nick Harrison and the other staff at Harvest House for their encouragement and confidence in this project. They had the foresight to understand and recognize that the truths contained in these pages and which have been useful in Bible studies for the past 25 years needed to be placed in the hands of more readers.

Thanks to Karen Vaughan and Andrea Mueller for their work on the typing and formatting of the manuscript. Bonnie Davidson and Molly Blass deserve special commendations for their countless hours of proofing, editing, collecting endorsements, and other tasks too numerous to mention. Not only did they assist me with excellence and professionalism, but they juggled many other demands on their time as this book was being developed.

I would be remiss if I did not specifically acknowledge Malissa Light for her help with this book. Malissa has a unique gift as a wordsmith and spent countless hours making this book easier to read, making me sound better, and ensuring my message was clear. I am grateful for her and indebted to her. Thanks, Malissa. I appreciate all your hard work very much.

Finally, I want to thank the Wednesday morning men's Bible study group of several years ago in which I participated for their prayers and encouragement as I developed this content.

Contents

Part 1: A Life Well Spent

Part 2: How to Get a Higher Return on Life

Part 3: How to Use Your Money More Effectively

Foreword

by Ron Blue

All Christians who are sincere in their faith long to stand before the Lord and hear Him say, "Well done, good and faithful servant; you were faithful over a few things, I will make you ruler over many things. Enter into the joy of the Lord." *Your Life... Well Spent* is written by a person who has a passion like few I know to live his life in such a way as to hear those words.

Russ has spent more than thirty years helping, coaching, encouraging, and challenging individuals and families to use all that God has entrusted them with for His glory and honor. Russ has been selfless in his passion.

The reality is that when you make *money* decisions, you make *life* decisions. Money and other financial resources are scarce for all of us, no matter how much we possess. As a consequence, all money is allocated to the real priorities of life. Money is a resource that God entrusts to us to be used in many different ways for the accomplishment of His plans and purposes. Ultimately, as those of us who are believers in the Lord Jesus Christ use the resources He has entrusted to us, we act as salt and light in a world that desperately needs to see proper models of lives that are balanced and well spent.

Russ has done a masterful job of dealing with some of the tremendous challenges people face in allocating their financial resources. For example, what is the trade-off between prosperity and posterity? This book answers that question in a way that is easy to understand but incredibly challenging to apply.

Believe me, you can trust the content of this book. It is built on probably more experience than almost anyone in this country has had in counseling and consulting with couples and individuals in the areas of money and money management. Russ understands very well the role that money plays in our lives.

You will find this book to be provocative, challenging, encouraging, practical, and, best of all, biblical. Russ Crosson is a man with a passion to share the practical outworkings of faith in the area of family and finances. I recommend this book without reservation.

—Ron Blue, founder, Ronald Blue & Co., LLC

PART 1

A Life Well Spent

A Glimpse of Eternity

A New Perspective on Money and Family

High up in the North, in the land called Svithjod, there stands a rock. It is 100 miles high and 100 miles wide. Once every 1,000 years a little bird comes to this rock to sharpen its beak. When the rock has thus been worn away, then a single day of eternity will have gone by.

HENRY WILLEN VAN LOON

In My Father's house are many mansions; if it were not so, I would have told you. I go to prepare a place for you. And if I go and prepare a place for you, I will come again and receive you to Myself; that where I am, there you may be also (John 14:2-3).

JESUS

It began as an uneventful Sunday morning. Jim had been calmly sitting in the third pew on the right-hand side of the Sunnydale Evangelical Church, a pew he and Barbara had warmed on and off for some twenty years. Pastor Firnbeck was preaching on rewards and eternity, his rich, vibrant voice filling the sanctuary as he recited 1 Corinthians 3:13-15: "Each one's work will become manifest; for the Day will declare it, because it will be revealed by fire; and the fire will test each one's work, of what sort it is. If anyone's work which he has built on it endures, he will receive a reward. If anyone's work is burned, he will suffer loss."

Jim's mind wandered as he pondered the great day when his turn for judgment would come and he would receive his reward. The words teased him to imagine vast riches: a mansion larger than the one he and Barbara occupied now, suits as well-fitting as those his tailor made for him (but these would be pure silk), a Mercedes to replace the BMW.

The sharp pain seemed to hit shortly after the little smile creased his lips. It came out of nowhere—though Jim would later think it came right from heaven—a bolt of electricity so powerful it sucked every molecule of air from his lungs. *Pain,* a word he knew little about but became intimately acquainted with in one split second, hit his chest and riveted down his arm. He could not scream. He could not move. He was alert, awake, yet unable to speak. There was a flurry of motion—Barbara calling his name, the pastor rushing down from the podium, Mrs. Monroe's large hat flying up. The words *ambulance, doctor, heart attack* flew past his ears, yet still that electrical pain held him in its grip.

What followed could only be described as reckoning day. The ride in the ambulance, the panic that filled his very soul, the awareness that judgment was no longer a fantasy about a day in the future but something that might take place within the next moment.

The hospital staff was efficient and quick; the pain relentless. Tubes and machines of every shape and size invaded his body, whirring, hissing, menacing.

An hour passed. Jim heard his name and tried to open his eyes but could not find the strength. Then he recognized his son's voice. Jimmy's questions to the nurse were pointed, cold, and emotionless: "How much longer does he have?"

"I'm sorry, but we've done everything we can possibly do for him."

"Do I have to stay around the hospital or could you just call me when he's gone?"

"Just leave your number at the desk, sir, and we will call you when there's a change."

Brisk, abrupt, businesslike, and uncaring, Jimmy's footsteps led to the door. Then his voice came again, as if he needed to explain. "I hardly know my dad. He was never home for us…always making a buck, always making a name. I…I…I'm sorry if I sounded abrupt."

What do you mean I was never there for you! You lived in the biggest house in the neighborhood, didn't you? You drove the fanciest car of any kid in your high school. And didn't you spend a couple of months touring Europe in the twelfth grade at my expense? The arguments screamed inside Jim's head. Then the anger turned to quiet-but-painful sobs that were lost to the whirring of the machines.

Time seemed shrouded in thick veils. Pastor Firnbeck was whispering above him. Barbara was there too; he could smell her rich perfume. She was crying. The minister was telling him the names of the twenty or so families who at that very moment were in the waiting room praying for him. Those families marched before his mind's eye. Several had some serious financial needs over the past few years, but he had never felt led to help in any way; he had been too busy. Pastor Firnbeck also talked of baskets of food already arriving at their home, of Joe Babcock flying his private plane to Philadelphia, 300 miles away, to pick up Jim and Barbara's daughter, Jill, so she could get to the hospital as soon as possible. Jim remembered that Babcock had asked him to contribute to a medical piloting ministry just six months before, but he'd thought it was a waste of money at the time—money now being lavishly spent on him.

Then a strange voice filled the room—a voice of authority, confidence—calling for a drug, explaining to Barbara the purpose and the hope. Jim could feel the needle entering his arm, then warm fluid entered his body, and his mind slowly lost its grip…going, going into twilight.

But this wasn't twilight. It was a waiting room. The carpet was red, royal red. Music (*Is it piped in?*) filled the room. Yet was it a room? Jim couldn't tell. He was sitting on a soft, comfortable sofa. Others were in the room, or so it seemed. He felt them, though he really couldn't focus on what they looked like.

"James Conwell." His name was being called, but he had no idea who was calling it. As he stood up, doors directly across from him opened, and he walked through. What met him was astounding. A room the size of...well, how could he even measure it? And it wasn't just the size. It was the awesome light. There was a throne. There was a robe, long and luxurious, filling up the entire room. There were strange creatures. Majesty and beauty. There was fear, and there was power. *There was God.* This was it...the day...this was no fantasy. This was reality.

Moments, hours, or perhaps years passed in silence. Jim couldn't tell. He couldn't think; he couldn't speak. The words came from the throne. The voice was love. "Jim, the time has come to test your life works," the voice said, booming—or was it whispering?—across the room. And then his life appeared: his first home, his first car, his marriage, his family's first car (he had forgotten that little green Plymouth), their first home, the 457-page project he had spent a year working on with six other coworkers, another home, tennis courts, a swimming pool, a fishing boat, more cars, membership at several exclusive clubs, twelve file cabinets full of papers—all his projects, his financial schemes, his investments—a summer home, a larger boat, his bank accounts. The pile grew and grew and grew.

Jim wondered how the room contained it all. He was awestruck by the impressive display before him. *I am wealthy beyond imagination,* he could hear his inner voice telling him, cheering him on. *Rich at last, rich for all eternity,* he almost sang under his breath.

Then the voice came again: "And now, Jim, the test of fire!" Where the fire came from, Jim had no idea. Though he was standing near the enormous pile, he was neither warmed nor singed by the blaze. But the fire came, and in one moment all was gone. *All was gone!*

Jim recalled the words read just that morning by Pastor Firnbeck: "If anyone's work is burned, he will suffer loss." Sixty-one years of life, all for one small pile of ashes. Jim could feel it before he actually heard it: deep sobs coming from his soul, weakening his knees, breaking his strength, flattening him out as he realized he had lived and worked all his life for nothing—absolutely nothing—of lasting value.

"Mr. Conwell." His name again, this time from a different voice. *Where am I?* The sound of whirring machines, the smell of perfume, the feel of the gurney under him, the nurse, Pastor Firnbeck with tears on his cheeks. He awakened from the dream for one more chance.[1]

A New Perspective on Money and Family

As the former CEO of the financial and investment advisory firm Ronald Blue & Co. (now Ronald Blue Trust), I have observed the tensions between money and family at all the various stages of life: The young couple starts out struggling with a budget, work pressures, and the demands of a growing family. The middle-aged corporate executive, entrepreneur, or doctor whose children are in their late teens begins to question whether his or her all-consuming work was worth it. The older couple approaches retirement and wonders what to do now.

These observations, as well as the current lack of "why to" (vs. "how to") books in the marketplace, have burdened me to write this book. The market is full of publications on financial planning, investments, debt, budgeting, and training your children, but I have yet to see a book that provides the broader context of *why* one should be interested in all those areas. This book is written to fill that gap. It's designed to be a primer to the other financial books. On one hand, this book is about money, but on the other hand, it is not about money at all. It's about money only in the context of something more important—your life and eternity.

Preparing for Eternity

To prepare for eternity, we must first have a keen awareness and a clear understanding that there will be a day of judgment for each of us. "And as it is appointed for men to die once, but after this the judgment"

(Hebrews 9:27). Many of us live as if there is no judgment, and consequently, we act as if it doesn't really matter how we live, especially after we trust Christ as our Savior. This seems to be a result of an unclear perspective on the two distinct judgments mentioned in Scripture.

One concept of judgment has to do with our sin. We will first be judged on whether we have accepted Christ's payment for our sin and by faith have trusted Him to be our Savior. If we accept Christ as Savior, our names will be found in the Book of Life (Revelation 20:12,15), we will enter heaven (John 1:12), and our sins will be remembered no more (Hebrews 10:17). If we have not personally trusted Christ, we will be cast into the lake of fire and will experience eternal separation from God (Revelation 20:15). (Note: If you have never trusted Christ as your Savior, see the appendix, "Spiritual Action Steps," at the end of this book to learn how you can do this.)

The second concept of judgment—and the one that should affect how we live our lives as believers—has to do with the judgment of our works.

Just as Jim Conwell dreamed, we will one day "appear before the judgment seat of Christ" where our works will be tested "according to what [we have] done, whether good or bad" (2 Corinthians 5:10). Salvation is by grace, not by works (see Ephesians 2:8-9). However, this second judgment is of our works and deeds, so it does matter how we live as believers. And since, unlike Jim, we usually don't get a second chance, our decisions today regarding money and family are critical in order to live an intentional life well spent.

In God's plan, the service of each of His children is scrutinized and evaluated (Matthew 12:36; Romans 14:10; Galatians 6:7; Ephesians 6:8; and Colossians 3:24-25). As a result of this judgment, there will be a reward or a loss of reward to the believer, as Pastor Firnbeck read from 1 Corinthians 3.

You may be thinking, *What difference does it make whether I have reward or loss of reward if I'm in heaven?* Scripture indicates, through phrases such as "more tolerable" (Matthew 11:20-24) and "greater condemnation" (Luke 20:45-47), that there are levels of judgment and reward. Our position of rulership or responsibility with Christ in heaven will be determined by how we live now. So it does matter how we live.

Once we understand that God is more concerned about the eternal than the temporal, we face some unique challenges in the financial area.

What are God's desires about how we live regarding our money and our family? The only place to find out is in God's handbook for life, the Bible. John 17:17 says, "Your word is truth." John 8:32 says, "You shall know the truth, and the truth shall make you free." What is important to God revolves around things that are eternal versus things that are temporal. "We do not look at the things which are seen, but at the things which are not seen. For the things which are seen are temporary, but the things which are not seen are eternal" (2 Corinthians 4:18). *Temporal* means "to last for a limited time or to be transient or provisional." *Eternal* means "to be ceaseless, everlasting, or endless."

Once we understand that God is more concerned about the eternal than the temporal, we face some unique challenges in the financial area of our lives. Why? Because so many of our decisions about money are temporal. Think about it. That newest technology quickly becomes obsolete. The freshly painted house soon needs painting again. The funds you saved for college are all used up.

As a matter of fact, all the "things" that can be done with money are temporal except for one: giving. If we give money to God's work, we will benefit personally with eternal rewards: "Not that I seek the gift, but I seek the fruit that abounds to your account" (Philippians 4:17). In addition, money used to support a missionary or a pastor has an eternal benefit because of the people he or she will impact, who in turn will impact others for eternity.

So, since most of what we spend our money on is going to be burned up, what is eternally significant? An often-quoted poem answers that question: "We have only one life, and it will soon be past; only what's done for Christ will last." The soul of mankind and the Word of God are all that will last. It follows, then, that only things that involve people or God's Word will not be burned up—our families, our neighbors, our prayers and fellowship, our godly character, our giving, and our witnessing, among others. Does this mean we shouldn't be concerned about money and possessions? No, not at all. Money is necessary and useful for buying food, shelter, clothing, and so forth while we are here on earth. But money and possessions will be of no benefit when we pass from this life to the next. "Riches do not profit in the day of wrath, but righteousness delivers from death" (Proverbs 11:4).

The choice, then, is between an eternal legacy that lasts or a legacy that does not last. Consider these words of Canadian real-estate baron Stephen Sander: "I'd make a $20 million deal and come home and say, 'This is insane. I need something for my soul. I'll leave behind a real legacy not just real estate.'"[2]

A Glimpse of Eternity

Knowing what is important to God helps us in our decision making about money and family, and it also helps us understand where we are ultimately going and how long we are going to spend there.

Christ has gone ahead to prepare a mansion for us (John 14:2); its size will be determined by the degree to which we accomplish God's business. We are going to heaven, which contains a city that is a solid cube—1500 miles by 1500 miles by 1500 miles (Revelation 21:10-27). These dimensions could mean 2,250,000 square miles on each tier of the cube extending 1500 miles upward—like a huge skyscraper. If each tier is one mile apart, the surface area of the city will be seventeen times larger than the surface of the earth, and fifty-eight times larger than the earth's land surface. It is a city made of gold and every precious stone—jasper, sapphire, emerald, chalcedony, sardonyx, sardius, chrysolite, beryl, topaz, chrysoprase, jacinth, and amethyst, not to mention the gates of pearls and transparent glass. As we think about heaven, our pursuit of earthly possessions should pale in comparison. We should have a desire for our families and others to be there. And that means we should be teaching our children to understand where they're headed and what is truly important in life.

Think again about the quote at the beginning of this chapter that describes a huge rock in the North, where every thousand years "a little bird comes…to sharpen its beak. When the rock has thus been worn away, then a single day of eternity will have gone by." Does that illustration grab you as it does me? I can comprehend living seventy, eighty, or even ninety years on earth, but I cannot begin to comprehend eternity. Yet that is where I am going to be soon. If I die before finishing this sentence or if I happen to live another forty or fifty years, either way eternity is coming *soon*. It is soon for you too. The key is to be ready.

That's why we want to make the right decisions today about our money and our families—so we will be positioned for our trip into eternity. As Randy Alcorn, pastor and author of many award-winning and bestselling books, said in his book *Money, Possessions, and Eternity*, "Someday this upside down world will be turned right side up, and nothing in all eternity will turn it back again. If we are wise, we will spend our brief lives on earth positioning ourselves for the turn."[3]

"Positioning ourselves for the turn." How do we do that? We do it by constantly focusing on the eternal (people) instead of the temporal (material possessions). All people are important to God, and consequently all people should be important to us. However, in this book we will focus on a strategic subset of all people—your family.

Many couples have expressed to me the sadness they feel that their children "just didn't turn out right," even though they gave them everything money could buy. Many marriages have experienced significant stress as a result of poor, short-term decisions about money. If we don't think long-term and see ourselves standing before God as Jim did, we will make short-term decisions that could have significant negative consequences in the future. As Ron Blue said, "The longer range your perspective, the better your decisions today." But why is it so difficult to think long-term about money?

I believe it has to do with the way we think. When my oldest son was three years old and someone would distract him, he didn't know how to say, "You made me lose my train of thought," so he would say, "You got my thinking off!" For many of us today, our thinking is off because we have subtly bought the lies of the world.

Let me illustrate. One of the first things we do to prepare a financial plan for an individual is to look at his or her tax return and ask for lists of assets and liabilities. When we ask whether there are any debts, it's not uncommon for the person to say, "No, except my home mortgage." My unspoken response is, *What do you call that if it is not debt?* We have become so used to having a home mortgage (it's "the American way" to have one) that we no longer consider it a debt. That type of thinking has come from the world's view of debt—not God's.

Although the Bible tells us "the borrower is servant to the lender" (Proverbs 22:7), the world tells us it's smart to get a loan. Bank commercials entice us to borrow so we can deduct the interest on our tax returns. After a while we begin to think we are losing out if we don't get a loan or "buy now, pay later."

Another illustration of worldly thinking versus biblical thinking is the concept of retirement. From the time we start working, we're programmed to think about quitting as soon as we can. Our focus is on making that "magic retirement time" happen as early as possible. We're urged by society to work long, hard hours, many times to the exclusion of our families, so that one day we won't have to work at all. Yet the Bible is clear about living a balanced life today, working and storing up treasures in heaven rather than on earth.

In the next few chapters we'll look at the difference between *prosperity*—the accumulation of goods on this earth—and *posterity*—the heritage we leave for the generations that come after us. Then in Part 2 we'll look at a new kind of balance sheet: the Life-overview Balance Sheet. We'll examine a unique definition of *capital* that includes our social and spiritual legacy, as well as the financial inheritance we leave our children. We'll examine our views on earning money in the context of the Life-overview Balance Sheet. Finally, in Part 3 we'll look at how we can best spend and invest our money to leave our desired social, spiritual, and financial legacies to our children.

As a fellow sojourner who grapples with these tensions, I hope you will be challenged as I was to think about money and our families. May this book be a resource to enable you to live a life well spent.

We will also look at the financial paradox of life: When we are young and need the money and a big house, we normally don't have them. But when the children are grown and have lives of their own, we can usually afford the large house and have more money than we've ever had. We'll look at the reasons why couples buy a big house just as the children leave and a big house is no longer needed. We will also consider the interesting fact that no one ever gets to the end of his or her life and says, "I wish I'd worked more and spent less time with my children."

At the end of the twentieth century we bid goodbye to the most prosperous century in history, when financial wealth was created and multiplied as never before. And other nations still look to America as a primary model for success. They want to accomplish what we have through increasing our standard of living. But what have we really accomplished?

We have increased our lifestyles, but in the process, have we lost our ability to really live? We have amassed wealth, not wisdom. We have given our children toys, not time. We have children who have been taught to consume rather than work. We have parents who don't know their children, and marriages that are strained or broken. We have been in a rush to run a race without understanding the finish line. Are we being robbed of our very lives because we're not thinking correctly about *why* we have money and *what* we are to do with it?

I realize some of the observations shared in these pages may offend some readers. That is not my intent. I also recognize that the observations and thoughts I share are not the only perspectives on life—work, finances, family, eternity, and so forth. However, as a fellow sojourner who grapples with these tensions, I hope you will be challenged as I was to think about money and our families. May this book be a resource to enable you to live a *life well spent*.

⌒ FOR FURTHER REFLECTION ⌒

1. Why is it so difficult in today's society to think in terms of the eternal?

2. Didn't Jim do a lot of "good" things during his life? Won't they count for something? Consider 1 Corinthians 3:13-15 in your answer.

3. What would you do differently if you knew your actions would really impact your rewards in eternity?

4. What comes to mind when you think of heaven?

5. How does an accurate, biblical view of heaven affect the way you live today?

Prosperity

The Accumulation of Goods

Measure wealth not by the things you have, but by the things you have for which you would not take money.
ANONYMOUS

Riches do not profit in the day of wrath, but righteousness delivers from death.
PROVERBS 11:4

I sometimes took my wife, Julie, and our children with me on business trips. One absolutely gorgeous fall day we took an overnight car trip to visit a prospective client. As we neared the address we'd been given, Julie was navigating with the scribbled directions in hand, and I was keeping my eyes peeled for signs of the house. We were getting further and further from the town where the new clients said they lived, but we hadn't come to the right address yet.

Then we saw it. What a magnificent place! Set back probably three-quarters of a mile off the road was a house that looked like it had come right out of *Southern Living* magazine. It was resplendent, especially with the leaves glistening in the autumn sun. As we drove down the winding lane with trees on each side, we could see what seemed to be dozens of thoroughbred horses grazing in the fertile pasture that surrounded the house and numerous outbuildings. Closer to the house, we could see a tennis court and gazebo off to one side, and a pool and cabana in the back near the barn. Julie and I agreed this was a dream setting.

It seemed obvious that the couple who owned this place must be extremely wealthy and successful, with riches beyond measure. As we were about to find out, however, that observation was false. We were actually more prosperous than they were!

"How is that?" you ask. It has to do with a *correct* or *biblical* understanding of prosperity, success, wealth, and riches. My purpose in this chapter is to clarify the definitions of these four words in light of God's Word so we can understand the fullness of their meanings, rather than limit them to the shallow context in which they're often used. Today's society uses these four words interchangeably, and in many cases synonymously. For example, we might say, "That person is wealthy" or "That person is successful" and mean the same thing. But do *wealthy* and *successful* really refer to the same thing?

Defining *Prosperity, Success, Wealth,* and *Riches*

To begin, let's look at the definitions of these words according to the original *Webster's Dictionary of the English Language,* considered by many to be a great authority in the field of American lexicography. Noah Webster struggled for most of his first fifty years with the issue of Christianity, until he finally realized his need for the saving power of Christ and became a Christian. This is important to note since almost all his definitions utilize God's written Word as a key to the meanings. He considered education useless without the Bible.[1]

Webster also understood that any age or society could destroy its language by changing the definitions. As a result, he defined basic words that were universal and had meanings that could not be disputed as a result of a secular or cultural change. In this context, the following words were defined:

- *Prosperity:* advance or gain in anything good or desirable; successful progress in any business or enterprise; success; attainment of the object desired. *Prosper:* to be successful; to succeed. *Prospering:* advancing in growth, wealth, or any good.

- *Success:* the favorable or prosperous termination of anything attempted; a termination that answers the purpose intended; prosperous, fortunate, happy.

- *Wealth:* prosperity, external happiness; riches; large possessions of money, goods, or land; that abundance of worldly estate that exceeds the estate of the greater part of the community; it is a comparative thing—a man may be wealthy in one place but not so in another.

- *Rich* or *Riches:* wealthy; opulent; possessing a large portion of land, goods, or money, or a larger portion than is common to other men or to men of like rank; an abundance of something; having more in proportion than our neighbors.

These definitions show that prosperity and success can be used synonymously because they both imply action or progress toward a desired end. Wealth and riches, on the other hand, can also be used synonymously because they are both comparative in nature and relate to material possessions and external things.

So do you want to be prosperous and successful or wealthy and rich? Was my prospective client prosperous or wealthy? By looking at these words as they relate to the world we live in, we can get a clue to the answer to this question.

The World's Definition of Prosperity

To understand how the world defines prosperity, we need only reflect on how we evaluate and think about other people. Have you ever been waiting for someone, and he or she drives up in a very nice new car? What was your immediate thought? If you're honest, I'm sure you'll admit thinking, *This person must be successful.* What about visiting a college friend you haven't seen in quite some time and you find his or her home in a nice subdivision? Don't you think he or she must be doing quite well to live there? Don't you think, *This person is prospering?* (This is what Julie and I thought as we approached the Southern-style mansion.) What if the neighborhood you are driving through is not so nice? Do you think, *Hmm, they aren't doing so well?* What about when you find out that the new member of your church is a doctor? *This person is a success,* right? Why? Because of what he or she does.

We think this way because the world has influenced us to believe prosperity and success are measured in one of three primary ways: material possessions, position (vocation), and power.

The world readily uses *material possessions,* such as cars, boats, houses, and nice clothes, to measure prosperity or success. When we see such things we make comments like "He has a successful company" or "She is successful" without any knowledge of the person's real financial condition or of how these things may have been obtained. As I've learned in my business, initial impressions can be very misleading. I've met with many individuals who drove expensive foreign cars and wore custom-made suits—and had more debts than assets. Their prosperous and successful appearance masked their debt.

If we use material possessions to measure prosperity or success, how do we view the affluent drug dealer or the crime kingpin? What about the young couple who receives a large inheritance? Are they successful? The world measures success more by perception than by reality. This means that, for many people, image is everything; accumulating things to look prosperous is the ultimate motivation in everything they do.

The second way the world measures prosperity or success is a person's *position* or *vocation.* Consider how you feel about a doctor, a lawyer, or an accountant versus a cook, a janitor, a missionary, or a schoolteacher. If you're honest, you will probably admit that you have not used the words *janitor, secretary, missionary,* and *success* in the same sentence recently. In the world, positions that generate the most income or require greater knowledge and education are the ones deemed successful, and vice versa. We tend to elevate knowledge without considering wisdom. We see this in how easily impressed we are by an individual's degrees from certain universities.

The third way to measure prosperity is *power.* We consider persons successful if they hold an office of power or authority. Consider the judge or the senator or the chief executive officer of a large corporation. In each of these positions the individual has the authority to make decisions and the power to carry them out. On the other hand, we do not consider nonleadership employees successful because they have very little control over their futures. Someone else is making decisions for them.

In God's economy a person is prosperous and successful as a result of the process he or she goes through in working, regardless of the fruit of that work.

When my first book, *Money and Your Marriage,* was published, I experienced firsthand the subtlety of the world's thinking on prosperity and success. After calling on a client in another town, I decided to visit a local Christian bookstore to see if they had my new book and to find out how many copies they had sold. Much to my surprise (as well as my chagrin), they had never even heard of my book! On the way home I happened to drive by another Christian bookstore in another small town. Being a glutton for punishment, I decided to stop and see how many they had sold. Again, they had never heard of it.

Why did I stop at those stores? Because I knew that in book

publishing, success is measured by the number of copies sold. If I was to be considered a success as an author, my book needed to sell a lot of copies. But is that true success?

It's obvious that the world has linked wealth and riches inextricably to success and prosperity. But how does God define these words?

God's Definition of Prosperity

Wealth, riches, and *prosperity* are not new terms. They are used many times throughout Scripture. For example, in Ecclesiastes 2:4-10 we read Solomon's words:

> I made my works great, I built myself houses, and planted myself vineyards. I made myself gardens and orchards, and I planted all kinds of fruit trees in them. I made myself water pools from which to water the growing trees of the grove...I had greater possessions of herds and flocks than all who were in Jerusalem before me. I also gathered for myself silver and gold and the special treasures of kings and of the provinces...So I became great and excelled more than all who were before me in Jerusalem...I did not withhold my heart from any pleasure, for my heart rejoiced in all my labor; and this was my reward from all my labor.

Solomon had it made. He was wealthy beyond measure. He had possessions, position, and power. "The weight of gold that came to Solomon yearly was six hundred and sixty-six talents of gold...So King Solomon surpassed all the kings of the earth in riches" (1 Kings 10:14,23). Let's take a closer look at Solomon's comments to gain insights into the differences between the world's definition of prosperity and God's definition. We will begin by examining the different meanings of possessions, power, and position.

The Process, Not the Possessions

Bill, a friend of mine, has very few possessions and lives quite modestly with his wife and four children in a small house on the other side of town. I met Bill at the urging of an acquaintance. He had just trusted Christ and was growing as a believer. Shortly after we met, Bill called to tell me he lost his job. Since that time, he has had several jobs, most of which have paid slightly more than minimum wage.

Though Bill is a talented, personable fellow, he just wasn't able to get a job that paid well. But through it all, I never heard him complain. He loves his wife and children and works hard to make sure there is food on the table. I cannot help but think of the mansion in heaven Bill will occupy.

In God's economy a person is prosperous and successful as a result of the process he goes through in working, regardless of the fruit of that work. In other words, if you do your work heartily and with the right attitude, you are a success regardless of your income level or what possessions you accumulate. Look at what Solomon said:

> Then I hated all my labor...Yet he will rule over all my labor in which I toiled...Therefore I turned my heart and despaired of all the labor in which I had toiled under the sun...
>
> There is nothing better for a man than that he should eat and drink, and that his soul should enjoy good in his labor. This also, I saw, was from the hand of God. For who can eat, or who can have enjoyment more than I? (Ecclesiastes 2:18-20,24-25).

Solomon realized the possessions his labor had produced actually amounted to nothing. The vineyards, silver, gold, flocks, and herds did not fulfill him. Though he may have appeared successful, he realized he was not. He knew if God did not give him the ability to enjoy the process of his labor, it was all vanity.

> He who loves silver will not be satisfied with silver; nor he who loves abundance, with increase...The sleep of a

laboring man is sweet, whether he eats little or much; but the abundance of the rich will not permit him to sleep (Ecclesiastes 5:10,12).

Here is what I have seen: It is good and fitting for one to eat and drink, and to enjoy the good of all his labor in which he toils under the sun all the days of his life which God gives him; for it is his heritage. As for every man to whom God has given riches and wealth, and given him power to eat of it, to receive his heritage and rejoice in his labor—this is the gift of God (Ecclesiastes 5:18-19).

There is an evil which I have seen under the sun, and it is common among men: a man to whom God has given riches and wealth and honor, so that he lacks nothing for himself of all he desires; yet God does not give him power to eat of it, but a foreigner consumes it. This is vanity, and it is an evil affliction (Ecclesiastes 6:1-2).

Thus, we see that the *process* of working is the real blessing. Success is found in the process, not in the product. As Henry Ford observed, "Work is the only pleasure. It is only work that keeps me alive and makes life worth living. I was happier when doing a mechanic's job."[2]

This means riches and wealth (material possessions in greater quantity than others around you) may be a curse or a blessing, depending on whether you have been empowered by God to enjoy them. Matthew Henry, in his *Commentary on the Whole Bible,* said:

Riches are a blessing or a curse to a man according as he has or has not a heart to make good use of them. God makes them a reward to a good man, if with them he gives him wisdom, and knowledge, and joy, to enjoy them cheerfully himself and to communicate them charitably to others. He makes them a punishment to a bad man if he denies him a heart to take the comfort of them, for they do nothing but tantalize him and tyrannize over him.[3]

Isn't it interesting that money, the very thing the world says makes people prosperous and successful, may actually be a curse? Does this mean money is evil and we shouldn't have it? No, money is not evil, and yes, a rich man can be successful. The key is God's empowerment. I believe God empowers us to enjoy the fruit of our labor by giving us the proper *perspective* about it. This perspective means we hold with open hands any material possessions that have come from Him. And remember: *Everything* we have comes from Him! "What do you have that you did not receive?" (1 Corinthians 4:7). We enjoy our possessions, but we don't let them own us. We express an attitude of "relaxed nonchalance" toward them, managing them enough to be good stewards without allowing them to consume us.

Too often, however, we do allow riches to consume us. It's been said that 95 percent of those who have been tested with *persecution* pass the test, but 95 percent of those who have been tested with *prosperity* fail. Perhaps this is why, in this prosperous country, we have one of the world's highest divorce rates, drug abuse in epidemic proportions, corruption in government, and increasing crime.

The first difference, then, between God's definition of prosperity and the world's definition is that godly persons who are prosperous have the ability to enjoy the labor God has given them to do, and they hold the fruit of that labor with open hands. You are prosperous living in a small house and driving an old car if you have God's perspective. Likewise, you are prosperous if you live in a large house and drive a new car as long as you hold them with an open hand.

If your attitude toward your possessions is not empowered by God, it doesn't matter what you earn or where you live. In an article in *Moody Monthly*, Dennis Haack wrote, "Abraham and Sarah were wealthy and they pleased God. Jeremiah was desperately poor, but no failure."[4] The trappings that money can buy have nothing to do with prosperity.

Character, Not Power

The second difference between God's definition and the world's definition of prosperity is His view of *power*. Instead of seeing power and authority as signs of prosperity and success, God sees *character* as the true indicator.

There is no greater place of power in the entire world than the office of the President of the United States. In elections, I find it interesting, however, that many of the American people are influenced by the place of power to the point of overlooking the character of the person who will occupy that office. It's incredible that the power of a presidential candidate can cause people to overlook his or her character—even if he or she might be immoral or ungodly.

God says character is what is important, not power. "The LORD does not see as man sees; for man looks at the outward appearance, but the LORD looks at the heart" (1 Samuel 16:7). If a person has power but is prideful, dishonest, disloyal, arrogant, driven, and greedy, he or she is not successful in God's eyes.

If a person is full of pride, any success that person may have in the world is invalidated by God. "God resists the proud, but gives grace to the humble" (1 Peter 5:5). The reason is that the attitude of pride believes "I have this power solely because of my ability," while the attitude of humility believes "God has given me this ability." Success results from character qualities such as integrity, honesty, teachability, loyalty, responsibility, courage, determination, endurance, hospitality, generosity, and humility.

We gain a clearer understanding of this definition by looking at the character quality of *humility*. The world says you are successful if you hold a place of power—managing partner, corporate executive, or elected official. God says if you want to be first, you should be last. If you want to be exalted on the day you move into eternity, you must exhibit humility now:

> But when you are invited, go and sit down in the lowest place, so that when he who invited you comes he may say to you, "Friend, go up higher." Then you will have glory

in the presence of those who sit at the table with you. For whoever exalts himself will be abased, and he who humbles himself will be exalted (Luke 14:10-11).

Therefore humble yourselves under the mighty hand of God, that He may exalt you in due time (1 Peter 5:6).

It is not false humility to say "I am no good," but humility that acknowledges total dependence upon a sovereign and almighty God. We understand that we live in His providence. When we understand God's definition of prosperity, we recognize that any honor or power that comes in this life is ultimately a gift from Him; He gets the credit. You can be a success to God while you're the president of the company or the number-one salesperson as long as you realize that what you are is a gift from Him.

Just as we can't measure success by possessions, neither can we measure success by power. The prophet Daniel is a good illustration of a person who was successful because of his character, not his power. Daniel was one of only a few Jewish youths whose character was such that they were put in the king's personal service. Daniel was elevated to a place of prominence, not because of his power (the king had the power), but because he was discerning, knowledgeable, humble, and thankful (see Daniel 1–6). In other words, Daniel was successful *because* of his character. Power can be fleeting, but character has staying power. As Albert Einstein once commented, "Try not to become a man of success but rather try to become a man of value."[5]

Obedience, Not Position

The final difference between God's definition and the world's definition of prosperity is God's view of *position*. Instead of seeing position as a symbol of prosperity and success, God sees obedience as the true indicator.

I once consulted with a young man who had followed his father and grandfather into the family business. He had a nice income, a nice house, nice cars, and all the extras. However, as I got to know him, I soon learned things were not as they appeared. The young man was actually miserable. He had been seeking counseling for quite some time, and his marriage was in trouble. As we worked through the situation, it was clear that he had not been obedient to God in choosing a vocation. He had followed in his father and grandfather's footsteps because that was the easiest path and he could make more money than if he started the new business he originally felt called to. Once he left the family business and started his own business, his life gradually came back into focus. He had less money, but he was content.

The world labeled this young man a success when he worked in the family business. Why? Because of the riches and material possessions he was able to accumulate as a result of his income. But was that the work God wanted him to do? Would this man be able to say to God what Jesus was able to say: "I have glorified You on the earth. I have finished the work which You have given Me to do" (John 17:4)?

We are all called to different vocations. We cannot all be doctors, developers, certified public accountants, or lawyers. We vitally need cooks, mail carriers, police officers, teachers, plumbers, printers, and truck drivers. Therefore, regardless of a person's vocation, only God really knows if he or she is successful. We do not and cannot know the degree of someone else's obedience. We can measure his or her wealth and riches, but not his or her success. People are only successful to the extent they are obedient to God's calling for them.

Is an excellent teacher who makes $40,000 a year less successful than a professional athlete who sits on the bench and makes $300,000 a month? According to God's definition, their obedience and the degree to which they have maximized the abilities He has given them are the keys to their success. Their income has nothing to do with it. They both could be failures if they are not doing their best or if they disobeyed God in choosing their vocation. Since God gives us the ability to make wealth (see Deuteronomy 8:16-18) and God designs each of us to perform different functions, then the income we earn cannot possibly be a true measurement of success. Dennis Haack summarized this idea in an article titled "Which Success Really Counts?":

> Wealth or poverty, fame or obscurity, power or helplessness, fulfillment or boredom—these are not the essence of life nor of spirituality. They are not the marks of success or failure. God calls us to faithfulness, to live a life of moment-by-moment trust and obedience in whatever circumstances He has ordained for us. We find true success only by faithfully knowing and doing the Word of God.[6]

The Successful Completion of "Right" Things

These issues of success and prosperity come together in the book of Joshua. One verse, in particular, contains God's definition of success:

> This Book of the Law shall not depart from your mouth, but you shall meditate in it day and night, that you may observe to do according to all that is written in it. For then you will make your way prosperous, and then you will have good success (Joshua 1:8).

We are successful when we are in the process of being obedient and carefully doing all that God's Word says to do. For example, I am successful as I train and love my children (Ephesians 6:4; Deuteronomy 6:6-8) and love my wife (Ephesians 5:28). These verses do not guarantee or promise financial blessings if we do what God's Word says. Rather, they free us up to realize that we can be successful whether or not we have money. Money is not the barometer! A successful person may or may not have money. Likewise, a person with money may or may not be a "success."

Do you remember the lesson I learned when looking in stores for my first book? The challenge for me was to realize that I was a success and prosperous *because I had been obedient to do what God had called me to do,* not due to how many copies of my book had sold.

Isn't that what Noah Webster said? He defined success as "the favorable or prosperous termination of anything attempted." In Joshua 1:8, the goals that are to be attempted come from God's Word. As we do these "right" things, we are successful. Does this mean that non-Christians cannot be successful? No, they have attempted and completed many endeavors benefitting mankind. The problem is that the successful endeavor may not have *eternal significance* for the nonbeliever on judgment day. It may benefit society, but it will be for naught when he or she stands before God. Obviously, then, success in God's economy is not just the successful completion of anything attempted but rather successful completion of *the right things*.

If we demoralize the definitions of success and prosperity and define them as products (cars, houses, boats, vacations, and so on) rather than as the process (obedience, character, and so forth), we will make temporal decisions instead of eternal ones.

What are the things we should do, whether in word or deed, that bring true prosperity to us and glory to God? As I've reflected on the Word and counseled hundreds of people, I've discovered three key areas related to money and family that matter in God's eyes.

The first is described in Colossians 3:23: "Whatever you do, do it heartily, as to the Lord and not to men." You are successful as you work hard at what God has called you to do, regardless of what your income is.

Second, "let nothing be done through selfish ambition or conceit, but in lowliness of mind let each esteem others better than himself" (Philippians 2:3). You are successful if you have harmony in your marriage and love your spouse and manage healthy relationships with others regardless of whether you have a place of power.

Finally, "[His saints] are preserved forever, but the descendants of the wicked shall be cut off. The righteous shall inherit the land, and dwell in it forever" (Psalm 37:28-29). You are successful as you train and love your children, regardless of your position.

"The real issue is redefining success, rethinking the basis of pleasure and fulfillment and practicing a life that builds that."[7] If we demoralize the definitions of success and prosperity and define them as products (cars, houses, boats, vacations, and so on) rather than as the process (obedience, character, and so forth), we will make temporal decisions instead of eternal ones. We will tend to sacrifice our families on the altar of material possessions. We will sacrifice relationships, including our marriages, in pursuit of position. We will sacrifice our character in the quest for power. We must rekindle the true definitions penned by Webster and eternally defined in Scripture to be truly prosperous and successful. We must pursue the biblical (correct) definition of prosperity rather than the false, shallow definition implied in wealth and riches.

We exhibit the correct understanding of prosperity, success, wealth, and riches when we use these words in a context that expresses the things God says are important: "He is a successful husband and father." "They have a prosperous family because their children have such good manners." "You are a successful wife and mother." And, conversely, if we see a Mercedes go by, we should think, *He has riches. I wonder if he is prosperous.*

What Julie and I didn't know as we drove toward that beautiful home I described at the beginning of this chapter was that the couple who lived there had riches, but they were not prosperous in the areas that mattered. It was a third marriage for both, and they had incredible challenges with their children, stepchildren, and their former spouses. And the litany went on and on. They would have gladly traded their gorgeous estate for something God says is much more important— *posterity.* In the next chapter we will look more closely at the heritage we leave to coming generations.

∼ FOR FURTHER REFLECTION ∼

1. Think about ways you use the words *success, prosperity, wealth,* and *riches.* In what context do you usually use them?

2. In what ways might your new understanding of the definitions of these words affect your day-to-day life?

3. What can you do to help your children understand the fullness of the true definitions rather than the narrow definitions that are so prevalent today?

4. Do you realize now that you are more successful than you thought before reading this chapter?

3

Posterity

The Heritage We Leave to Coming Generations

Children are the living messages we send to a time we will not see.

J.W. WHITEHEAD

A family is the caretaker of the soul of man.

"ESTATE SALE" VIDEO, WHITE LION PICTOGRAPH PRODUCTIONS

The future is purchased by the present.

SAMUEL JOHNSON

Behold, children are a heritage from the LORD, the fruit of the womb is His reward. Like arrows in the hand of a warrior, so are the children of one's youth. Happy is the man who has his quiver full of them.

PSALM 127:3-5

A s I walked off the plane one Sunday afternoon, I quickly scanned the airport sign for directions on where I should go to meet my clients. They were flying their private, four-seat plane to take me to their home 150 miles away. I quickened my pace as I spotted arrows pointing to the terminal for private and commuter aircraft. I knew they would be waiting for me, and sure enough, as I walked across the tarmac to the plane, Jim Montague and his dad, Paul, came forward to greet me.

Paul, then in his early seventies, had started a small manufacturing business several years earlier and was still active in the business, along with Jim, who was in his forties. They were clients, and over the years we had become good friends while maintaining a strong client/adviser relationship.

When they realized the entire Montague family was going to be together for an upcoming family reunion, Jim and Paul decided it would be beneficial if I would come and share with the group the financial principles I had helped them implement in their business. As the small, single-engine plane swooped low over the cornfields and the barn next to their home to land on the grass-covered runway, I had no idea what I was about to observe.

At least 100 people representing four generations were at this family reunion. As I mingled through the happy throng, meeting many of the family members, I noticed a unity and harmony that's rare to see. I was especially impressed with the relationships between the generations. The children and adults interacted in a very mature and respectful manner, seeming to genuinely enjoy each other. The jet skis on the small lake next to the house were in constant use, with the older kids and adults helping the younger children. The food spread on tables under the shade trees provided a setting for wide-ranging conversations as the family members ate together. *What*, I wondered, *is behind the interactions I am observing? Why does this family get along so well?* I decided to ask Paul, the patriarch of the group. After all, at that time I was just beginning my own family and I welcomed his advice.

Paul explained to me that in six generations of Montagues there had been eleven ministers, four lay ministers, fifteen music ministers, twenty Sunday school teachers, seven missionaries, seven professors, seventeen school teachers, and twelve Christian college students.

What a heritage! I thought. *What is the secret to ensuring that generation after generation will pass on the essentials for leading lives that count for eternity?* When I asked Paul this question, he motioned for me to follow him into the house, where he pulled an old book from a shelf in his library and dusted off its cover. He flipped a few pages and stopped.

He handed it to me and said, "Russ, this is the key to what you see out here today." On the page were words spoken by his grandfather, Daniel Montague, more than 100 years ago, on August 2, 1882. At the age of seventy-seven he had addressed a similar family reunion, telling his loved ones:

> Now if you wish those principles established and carried out by your descendants, inculcate into the minds and hearts of your children the principles of religious instruction. Everything, almost, that is evil, everything, almost, to subvert the religion of Jesus Christ, is at work; and it is absolutely necessary to train the rising generation in the principles of Christ. It is the great work of the country. For Christian institutions, friends, we have reason this day to thank God; and what I ask of you who are now on the stage of action is that you should be true to the principles of Christ and humanity, to the name and characteristics of the Montagues that have gone before you.

There was the key: the rising generations. *The children!* What I observed at this family reunion was a family's *godly posterity.* Their unity and harmony were the results of a focused plan to pass on Christ's principles from one generation to the next. And the only way these principles could have gotten from Daniel Montague in 1882 to the young children playing before me that Sunday afternoon was for succeeding generations to do their part while they were on their "stage of action."

As I left the family gathering the next day, I was struck with the irony that although I had gone to the Montagues to share financial principles and talk with them about money, they had shared with me a principle that was much more important: *the principle of posterity.* As I thought about that day, I realized that I, like most people I know, did not seem to be very interested in posterity. I spent more time being concerned about my finances than posterity. Why?

I believe the reason financial wealth has replaced posterity in our thinking is twofold. First, as we discussed in the last chapter, the world does not know the true definition of prosperity. We have falsely defined prosperity as "money," and we have pursued that goal rather than true prosperity—godly posterity.

Second, like the world, we do not know the real definition of posterity. As I share its definition in this chapter, my hope is that you will come to realize, as I did, that money is simply a tool to invest in our posterity.

Posterity Defined

Posterity is defined in Webster's dictionary as "descendants; children, children's children…indefinitely; the race that proceeds from a progenitor." *Posterity, then, is our descendants—our children and grandchildren.*

At this point you could conclude that this book has nothing for you if you are single or do not have children. To the contrary! If you think of posterity as people you may influence for eternity, then these principles apply to you just as easily as they apply to a married couple with children or grandchildren. When you see the term *children,* think of the individuals you are discipling or influencing and remember that God is concerned about people—*all* people. Therefore, if you impact people through discipleship and a godly influence, you have posterity in the family of God and the principles apply.

Understanding that *posterity* is really the only mark I can leave on the generations that come after me has changed the way I look at money and possessions. Many people start their business careers with the objective of creating a name for themselves and leaving a mark on society by making a lot of money and becoming a recognized figure in the community. Many persons even hope to have their names on a building or two as a lasting tribute to their contribution to society. But before setting those kinds of goals, let's look at some Scripture verses for perspective:

> Their inner thought is that their houses will last forever, their dwelling places to all generations; they call their lands after their own names. Nevertheless man, though in honor, does not remain; he is like the beasts that perish (Psalm 49:11-12).

> Do not be afraid when one becomes rich, when the glory of his house is increased; for when he dies he shall carry nothing away; his glory shall not descend after him. Though while he lives he blesses himself (for men will praise you when you do well for yourself), he shall go to the generation of his fathers…A man who is in honor, yet does not understand, is like the beasts that perish (Psalm 49:16-20).

> The day of the Lord will come as a thief in the night, in which the heavens will pass away with a great noise, and the elements will melt with fervent heat; both the earth and the works that are in it will be burned up (2 Peter 3:10).

These words make it clear that it is impossible for us to leave a lasting mark through material means. The only mark that will truly last is our posterity. This concept is vividly illustrated by the first-century disciples. These men did not leave material things as their mark in history; their legacy is that Christianity is alive and well more than 2000 years after they lived.

The Bible on Posterity

As I've studied this concept of posterity, I've been amazed at how many times the Bible uses words that are related to posterity, such as *descendants*. The following verses should help you understand the emphasis the Bible puts on pursuing posterity instead of financial wealth:

> Who is the man that fears the LORD? He will instruct him in the way he should choose. His soul will abide in prosperity, and his *descendants* shall inherit the land (Psalm 25:12-13 NASB).

> I have been young, and now am old; yet I have not seen the righteous forsaken, nor his *descendants* begging bread (Psalm 37:25).

> For the LORD loves justice, and does not forsake His saints; they are preserved forever, but the *descendants* of the wicked shall be cut off. The righteous shall inherit the land, and dwell in it forever (Psalm 37:28-29).

> Mark the blameless man, and behold the upright; for the man of peace will have a *posterity.* But transgressors will be altogether destroyed; the *posterity* of the wicked will be cut off (Psalm 37:37-38 NASB).

> Let his *posterity* be cut off, and in the generation following let their name be blotted out. Let the iniquity of his fathers be remembered before the LORD, and let not the sin of his mother be blotted out. Let them be continually before the LORD, that He may cut off the *memory* of them from the earth (Psalm 109:13-15).

> Tell your children about it, let your children tell their children, and their children *another generation* (Joel 1:3).

> The *memory* of the righteous is blessed, but the name of the wicked will rot (Proverbs 10:7).[1]

Many principles can be drawn from these verses, but two stand out. First, every person will have a posterity. We all leave some kind of influence and mark on the next generation. The question is, "What type of posterity will you leave?" Second, a righteous, godly posterity will last forever, but a wicked posterity will not be remembered.

The legacy of our posterity…is determined to a large degree by the decisions we make today while we are on the "stage of action."

You may be thinking that a wicked posterity *can* last from generation to generation. "One generation of thieves leads to another." And that is true. But in the end, *when eternity comes,* the righteous will inherit the earth and the wicked will be remembered no more.

The legacy of our posterity (whether righteous or wicked) is determined to a large degree by the decisions we make today while we are on the "stage of action." The sobering fact is that we don't get a second chance to be on stage. As we go through life, we must choose whether to focus primarily on the pursuit of money and the things money can buy or on a godly posterity.

These two paths are not always mutually exclusive, and success is defined as learning the balance between them. We will discuss this balance throughout this book; but in too many cases we have bought into the world's definition of prosperity to the detriment of our posterity.

Anyone can leave a mark on the next generation, regardless of his or her income, position, or possessions. How? By inculcating into the minds of his or her children the "principles of Christ." As Daniel Montague said, "To do this, we must know what these principles are; they must come from the Bible." If we don't use the Bible as our standard, we will, by default, teach our children the ways of the world. The world's way of thinking could result in unhealthy marriages for our children. They could be taught to think that money is the key to happiness, encouraged to pursue jobs only for the money they will earn, and delegate to others the job of raising their posterity while they pursue power and wealth.

The Big Picture

In these first three chapters we have seen that we're truly prosperous and successful only as we leave a godly posterity. We have clearly seen from Scripture that money and material possessions will not last, but that our posterity will. We have also learned that the type of posterity we leave is determined by the decisions we make during our lives, and in life we get only one shot to craft our legacy.

In Part 2 we will look at how we can get a higher return on life and still handle our money wisely.

⟋ For Further Reflection ⟋

1. Are your words consistent with your actions? If not, what changes do you need to make in your life to be consistent?

2. Write something you would like to say to a reunion of your posterity 100 years from now.

3. What steps do you need to take to maximize your effectiveness during your remaining years?

Part 2

How to Get a
Higher Return on Life

4

The Life-overview Balance Sheet

*Distribution of Our Financial,
Social, and Spiritual Capital*

*Maybe a lesser return on your investments makes
sense in exchange for a higher return on your life.*
DICK DAVIS DIGEST

*Then I hated all my labor in which I had toiled
under the sun, because I must leave it to the man
who will come after me (Ecclesiastes 2:18).*
SOLOMON

J ulie and I are the proud parents of three sons: Clark, Reed, and Chad. As we faced the challenge of determining how much time I should spend working, how quickly I should amass money for retirement (if at all), and so forth, we spent much time discussing what our involvement in the church should be, and how—if any—our involvement should change as the kids matured through the years. On top of this, we wanted to model a good work ethic for our boys while still finding time to spend with them while they were young and most impressionable.

51

Understanding the correct definitions of *wealth, prosperity, success,* and *riches* is helpful, and we should all desire godly posterity. But how does this all work out in everyday life? How do we get a "higher return on life" and still handle our money wisely? How do we balance the demands of life?

The Life-overview Balance Sheet on the next page depicts the integration of the two concepts we have been developing: money and family or financial prosperity and posterity.

Understanding the Balance Sheet

The line at the top of the diagram represents our lives. Each of us has been given a certain amount of time, short or long, to be here on Earth. We must maximize this time, consistently seeking what God says is important. Two of my favorite verses speak to this need to live purposefully:

> Look carefully then how you walk! Live purposefully and worthily and accurately, not as the unwise and witless, but as wise—sensible, intelligent people; making the very most of the time—buying up each opportunity—because the days are evil (Ephesians 5:15-16 AMP).

> And this I pray, that your love may abound yet more and more and extend to its fullest development in knowledge and all keen insight—that is, that your love may display itself in greater depth of acquaintance and more comprehensive discernment; so that you may surely learn to sense what is vital, and approve and prize what is excellent and of real value—recognizing the highest and the best, and distinguishing the moral differences (Philippians 1:9-10 AMP).

As we live out our lives, the challenge is to be involved in the areas God says are important (the areas in the wheel on the left side of the diagram). We know from Scripture that church attendance is important. We are not to forsake our assembling together (Hebrews 10:24-25). We

FIGURE 4.1

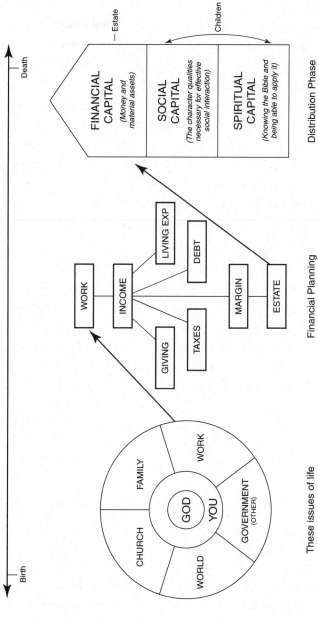

The Life-overview Balance Sheet

Birth — Death

FINANCIAL CAPITAL
(Money and material assets)

SOCIAL CAPITAL
(The character qualities necessary for effective social interaction)

SPIRITUAL CAPITAL
(Knowing the Bible and being able to apply it)

— Estate

Children

Distribution Phase

WORK

INCOME

GIVING — TAXES — LIVING EXP — DEBT

MARGIN

ESTATE

Financial Planning

CHURCH — FAMILY — WORLD — GOVERNMENT (OTHER) — WORK

GOD — YOU

These issues of life must be balanced.

know we are to be "salt and light in the world" (Matthew 5:13-16), and at the same time we're to work hard (Colossians 3:23) to provide for our families (1 Timothy 5:8) and spend time with them (Deuteronomy 6:6-8). We know that posterity is of utmost importance to God, and that material possessions, though part of our lives, are not vital to God and do not have eternal value.

I have observed, however, that in spite of knowing these truths, most people (Christians included) are working hard, fast, and long in the pursuit of a prosperity defined by money and possessions (including funding the spending areas listed in the middle section of the diagram), only to realize toward the end of their lives, when they plan the distribution of their money and possessions (the Financial Capital on the right), that they didn't adequately train their posterity—their children—to handle that capital.

The house on the right side of the diagram represents our children (posterity) and the three forms of capital—spiritual, social, and financial —that we will leave to them. If you do not have children, you leave these three components to those you have discipled during your lifetime. Let's take a closer look at these types of capital.

Spiritual Capital, or spiritual resources, includes an understanding of biblical absolutes—of how to come to Christ, of God's character, of how to walk by faith and trust God. It also includes the biblical principles of money management, raising children, marital relationships, and so forth. Spiritual capital is the ability to know and apply the Bible to our lives. It's using the absolute truths of God's Word to determine right from wrong, good from evil.

Social Capital is a resource base that allows us to relate to society. All the character qualities necessary for effective and productive interaction in society are part of a person's social capital. For example, responsibility is a necessary trait to hold a steady job, as are punctuality, honesty, integrity, loyalty, and discipline. Ethics are a critical component of social capital and includes morality, conformity to rules of right conduct, and distinguishing right from wrong.

Let me illustrate how spiritual and social capital are integrated. We know from the Word of God (spiritual capital) that work is commanded (2 Thessalonians 3:10), a gift (Ecclesiastes 5:18-19), is good (Genesis 2:5,15), and is to be done heartily (Colossians 3:23). These truths are lived out in the social capital arena as one works heartily for his or her employer, exhibits a strong work ethic, and is a productive, contributing member of society.

Financial capital is money and material assets, such as real estate, stock, and jewelry. By wisely balancing all aspects of life early (including our careers), we maximize time to invest in the spiritual and social capital of our posterity. Further, the financial capital we have amassed will be for naught if the other forms of capital are not present in the lives of our families.

All the spiritual and social training that goes on in our posterity is behind the scenes. It cannot be measured on a balance sheet and observed like our financial capital.

The best way to illustrate the integration of money and family is to think of the house in the diagram as a physical home. The foundation of the house represents *spiritual* and *social* capital, and the house itself represents the *financial* capital. Who would build a house without a solid foundation? That would be foolish. Yet many people are busy building financial houses (working to make more money) and neglecting the all-important foundation (their families).

Interestingly, the foundations of most real houses cannot be seen.

Similarly, the spiritual and social training that goes into our posterity takes place behind the scenes. It can't be measured on a balance sheet and observed like financial capital. Remember what 2 Corinthians 4:18 says: "We do not look at the things which are seen, but at the things which are not seen. For the things which are seen are temporary, but the things which are not seen are eternal."

One final observation about the foundation: It cannot be constructed by an absentee builder. Jesus trained His disciples by being with them: "He appointed twelve, that they might *be with Him* and that He might send them out to preach" (Mark 3:14). To train our children, we must spend time with them. Spiritual and social capital cannot be built into our children except by spending time with them. And this doesn't mean just quality time but *quantities* of time.

Unfortunately, many parents fail to recognize the impact of being absent from their children until much later in life, when they're planning their estate and specifying the distribution of their financial capital. Just as older concrete and boards are less pliable and moldable, so are children when they are older and more set in their ways. That's why it is essential (although admittedly difficult) to balance the issues on the Life-overview Balance Sheet throughout your family's life together. From the beginning, in addition to financial capital, parents should continually build spiritual and social capital at every opportunity.

The Challenge

Life rarely comes easy. It's a challenge to balance the need to earn a living (provision) with the goal of training and impacting our posterity. One difficulty is that our posterity's most urgent need for us comes at the exact time our income needs are greatest and the time pressures from our work are the most demanding. We have heard it said that the most strategic time for raising up our children is during their first ten years, when the majority of the training and instruction in their values takes place. This also happens to be the time most parents begin their careers and have the greatest time pressures at work.

When we need the time, money, and the big house for the children, we don't have it to give them. And when we finally get the time, money, and the big house, we don't need them. The children have started families of their own.

Too often the career pressures win the tug-of-war. As William R. Mattox notes, "Curiously, American families currently devote greater hours to paid work during the state in life when they are most apt to have childrearing responsibilities and fewer hours (if any at all) during the twilight years of life (between ages 55 and 70) when they are least apt to have dependent care duties."[1]

It all seems backward, doesn't it? When we need the time, money, and a large house for the children, we don't have it to give them. And when we finally have the time, money, and a large house, we don't need them. The children have moved out and started lives of their own.

We encounter two risks when we don't accept the challenge of living a balanced life. First, we could get to the end of our lives only to discover we have financial capital but no relationship with our posterity. The life of J. Paul Getty, the well-known millionaire who died in 1976, illustrates the consequences of this risk.

- The rich oil king once said that he would have sacrificed his entire fortune in exchange for a successful marriage. He... made five attempts at marriage.

- His millions...bought him neither peace nor tranquility of mind. He once said that there are a lot of things that money cannot buy. It could not buy health, nor affection, nor good digestion, nor a long life. He also said that money could be an obstacle to happiness.

- Several of his wives said they could not share the life of a man devoured by a passion for business.

- Some of his children [were] against him. His grandson was [kidnapped].[2]

The second risk we take if we don't balance our lives is that our children will be ill-prepared to handle what we have worked to accumulate for them if we don't teach them how to manage it. As a result, we could feel as Solomon did, recognizing that it all is vanity (Ecclesiastes 2:18-21).

Years ago I met a gentleman whose lament echoed Solomon's. As we visited, it was obvious he had been quite successful at amassing financial capital but very unsuccessful at building spiritual and social capital into his children. As a matter of fact, for some time their relationship had been strained to the point that they barely spoke to one another. He wanted to leave his financial assets to them, but they didn't want to have anything to do with him or his possessions.

He admitted that he had seldom been around while his children were young, and he acknowledged that some of the current friction was a result of his absence. His business schedule called for him to leave home on Monday and return on Friday. When he was at home, the perfectionist expectations he placed on his children alienated them from him.

I wish this scenario was a rare exception, but my observation is that it is all too common. At the beginning of the twenty-first century, a tremendous amount of financial capital resided in the hands of the post-World War II generation (some reports put this figure at six to eight trillion dollars). As these assets have been passed on to the baby-boomer generation and their children, most have been ill-prepared to receive it. They were not trained in how to manage it because their parents were too busy earning that money. To compound the problem, the baby boomers were so busy chasing the same false definition of prosperity as their parents did (money and possessions) that they neglected to train their children on how to use those assets.

Right now you face three challenges, regardless of whether you are just beginning your family and career, you are now in the thick of it, or you are like the elderly gentleman who was trying to sort out his estate for his uninterested children:

- The challenge to *balance life* while earning your money. (We'll discuss this in more detail in chapter 6.)
- The challenge to use money wisely and make good financial decisions to *free up time* to invest in your posterity (to be discussed in chapter 7).
- The challenge to *strategically invest* the time you've freed up (to be discussed in chapters 8–13).

As you study these chapters, I hope the words of Socrates ring in your head as they do in mine: "What mean you fellow citizens, that you turn every stone to scrape wealth together and take so little care of your children to whom you must one day relinquish it all?"

⌒ FOR FURTHER REFLECTION ⌒

1. What are some of the challenges you face in balancing work and family?

2. Why do you think God allows the existence of the time tension we face in the early years of our families? Why don't we have the money earlier in life when we need it, rather than later in life when we don't need it?

3. In what ways are you scraping wealth together, as Socrates said, to the exclusion of your children to whom you must one day relinquish that wealth?

The Principle of Time Replacement

How to Add Posterity Time to Our Schedules

Did you ever see a tombstone with a dollar sign on it? Neither did I. I have known hundreds of men who lived as though their only ambition was to accumulate it, but I have never known one who wanted a final judgement of himself to be based on what he got. A man wants people to read in his obituary, not a balance sheet of his wealth but a story of his service to humanity.

HOMILOPE

The days of our lives are seventy years; and if by reason of strength they are eighty years, yet their boast is only labor and sorrow; for it is soon cut off, and we fly away...So teach us to number our days, that we may gain a heart of wisdom.

PSALM 90:10,12

Years ago at one of our client conferences, Dr. James Dobson, a noted authority on the family, made an interesting comment: "If a couple loses their kids, they have nothing." He went on to say that the greatest threat to the family, and subsequently the greatest contributor to losing our posterity, is having no time.

I agree with his assessment, and believe that unwise financial decisions can compromise your time. In chapters 6 and 7 we will look at how financial decision making affects time. But first let's look at the subject of time—the critical component to leaving a godly posterity.

What Is Time?

In his book *Living on the Ragged Edge,* Chuck Swindoll defines time as "a stretch of duration in which things happen."[1] Our lifetime is the "stretch of duration" we have in which to make things happen. The challenge is to make things happen with our posterity instead of with wealth and material possessions.

Regardless of whether we are rich or poor, we all have the same amount of time in a day. We all have twenty-four hours in each day to spend as we choose. Once it's gone, each increment of time is irretrievable; it cannot be repeated or relived, which is why strategic use of our time is so critical. We want to do the right things with it—the eternal things, the purposeful things.

Leon Danco, an internationally recognized authority on the management of family-owned businesses, made this statement in his book *Beyond Survival:*

> A working lifetime is less than 500 months. Every time we take off one of those monthly watchband calendars and throw it away, we are throwing away an increasing percent of what is left. That realization is sobering. Time is not recallable. No warranties, no inventory, no quality assurance, no return of the deposit. Time just runs out...Time is our most finite and irreplaceable resource.[2]

Buying Time

Each day we all have the same amount of time to allocate among the various issues of life—work, family, ministry, and the world. We also have the same opportunities to "buy time" for investment in our posterity. Let me illustrate.

An extra amount that is not committed to a specific purpose is called *margin.* So when we refer to the concept of "buying time," we are talking about building margin. In most homes, people have used their money to buy time-saving appliances, such as instant pots and robotic vacuums. Doing this frees up time that can be directed toward other interests. Outside, many of us pay a lawn service to free us from weekends spent in the yard. We have used our cash to buy the margin of time.

There is a fine line between indulging our children and using our money to invest in memories and create closeness.

The critical question is how do we use the "free time" or time margin these conveniences create? Is it directed toward the social and spiritual capital of our posterity or toward other pursuits? All too often, instead of using this "bought" time for training our children and modeling godly priorities for others, we spend more time working in the pursuit of more money or we buy more possessions that require time to use and maintain. As a result, the typical full-time employee's work week has expanded from forty to nearly fifty-seven hours.[3] Technology has increased our accessibility and allows us to work anywhere anytime, which is a blessing and a curse. We must be more cognizant than ever that we are using our time wisely and ensuring our family time is focused and distraction-free whenever possible. Instead of working or acquiring more, it is critical that we use the time margin we've created to focus on what God says is important—our posterity.

Years ago, Julie and I chose to use some of our savings to renovate our basement to provide a greater play area for the children. We also decided to cement a portion of the yard and put up a basketball court so the boys and I had a place to play ball, something I hoped would help me stay emotionally close to them as they grew. We also used some extra money to do things with the boys on weekends: attending football games, going ice skating, playing miniature golf, and so on. Although some people might call these items living expenses, I see them as investments in my posterity.

When our three children were all under six years old, we allocated some money for a housecleaning service to buy Julie more time to invest in the kids. For a couple of years this was a good investment. It freed her to do the things she needed to do with the children. However, once the children were in school, we no longer invested money that way.

Some people may find they need to invest in a lawn service so they can free up time to spend with their young children rather than spend all weekend working in the yard. If the children are old enough to do some of the work, maintaining the yard as a family can teach a good work ethic, and a lawn service may not be a good investment. The key is to use our money wisely to buy time—not things—unless, of course, the things enhance the time (as appliances and lawn services can do, for example). We need to be creative and resourceful in our thinking in this area, taking into account our station in life and the ages of our children.

There is a fine line between indulging our children and using our money to invest in memories and create closeness. The point to consider is that money is a *tool*, and when it's used to create time that can be spent training our children, that's potentially a much better investment than putting the money in the bank or the stock market so we can retire sooner. I'm not suggesting that you shouldn't look ahead and build financial resources for the future. But I encourage you to realize that money is utilitarian, and in addition to stocks, bonds, and real estate, some of it can and should be invested in the higher priority of rearing godly posterity. The amount and manner in which this is done is a matter of prayerful consideration between husband and wife. When you make spending decisions, ask, "How will this expense affect our entire family?"

It's important to realize that it costs more today to buy time than it did when the family wasn't so fragmented. In past decades, a young couple's extended family provided free help with such things as baby-sitting and loaning of tools (grandpa's nearby shop was stocked, so other family members didn't need to buy equipment). Today it's still possible to buy time without money, for example, swapping babysitting time and sharing tools with trusted friends and neighbors, but it's much more difficult than it used to be. We need to manage our money wisely so we have resources available to "buy" the time we need for our families.

Obstacles That Steal Time

Just as we can use our money to buy time to invest in posterity, four major obstacles can steal the time we plan to spend with our posterity. These four obstacles are our inability to say no, our inability to slow down, our inability to turn off technology, and our inability to control our desire for possessions. Let's take a closer look.

Our Inability to Say No

Dennis Rainey, the founder of FamilyLife Ministry, has said that the word *no* may be the most powerful word in the English vocabulary. Powerful, I agree, because it has the greatest potential to affect the balance in our lives—positively or negatively.

It's impossible to live balanced lives and make wise use of our time if we don't say no to a lot of "good" things. Having the ability to say no means we've thought through what is eternally important, and we've set goals for our family, ministry, work, and involvement with the world. These goals are unique to each individual; they form the grid through which all decisions are made. Parents need to use these nine words frequently to buy time: "No, that is not on our list of priorities!"

As Richard Swenson said in his book *Margin*, "To be able to say no without guilt is to be freed from one of the biggest monsters in our overburdened lives. If we decline, not out of self-serving laziness but for God-honoring balance and health, this level of control will not only protect our emotional margin (and time) but will actually increase it."[4]

I remember when our first child was born. A friend commented that we were going to be "out of pocket" for the next six years. It didn't take us long to understand what she meant, especially when our other children came along. During that stage in our lives—when our boys were babies and toddlers—they demanded so much of our physical time we had to say no to a lot of good things, such as teaching Sunday school, that we had enjoyed in the past.

Julie and I concluded that if we were to keep some time in our schedules to strategically build spiritual and social capital into our children (something we call "posterity time") we needed to practice the *Principle of Replacement*. (The chart on the next page illustrates this concept.) It means we would only add new projects or commitments to our schedule if they replaced something else in our schedule. (This assumes that we have a schedule that is balanced and not too busy to begin with.)

Note that in the Principle of Replacement chart a balanced schedule includes time for Bible study and activities (such as kids' sports and school programs), plus time for sleeping, dressing, eating, exercising, and work, as well as unaccounted-for or unscheduled time and time available for posterity. Although I may share some activities, including Bible study, with my children, I still need to have some unplanned posterity time in my schedule.

I can sleep less, forego exercise, or neglect my spiritual time to create posterity time, but in the long run if I get my posterity time from these timeslots I will be too tired to share with my children. And, besides that, I'll have nothing left to share. Therefore, the addition of new time

FIGURE 5.1

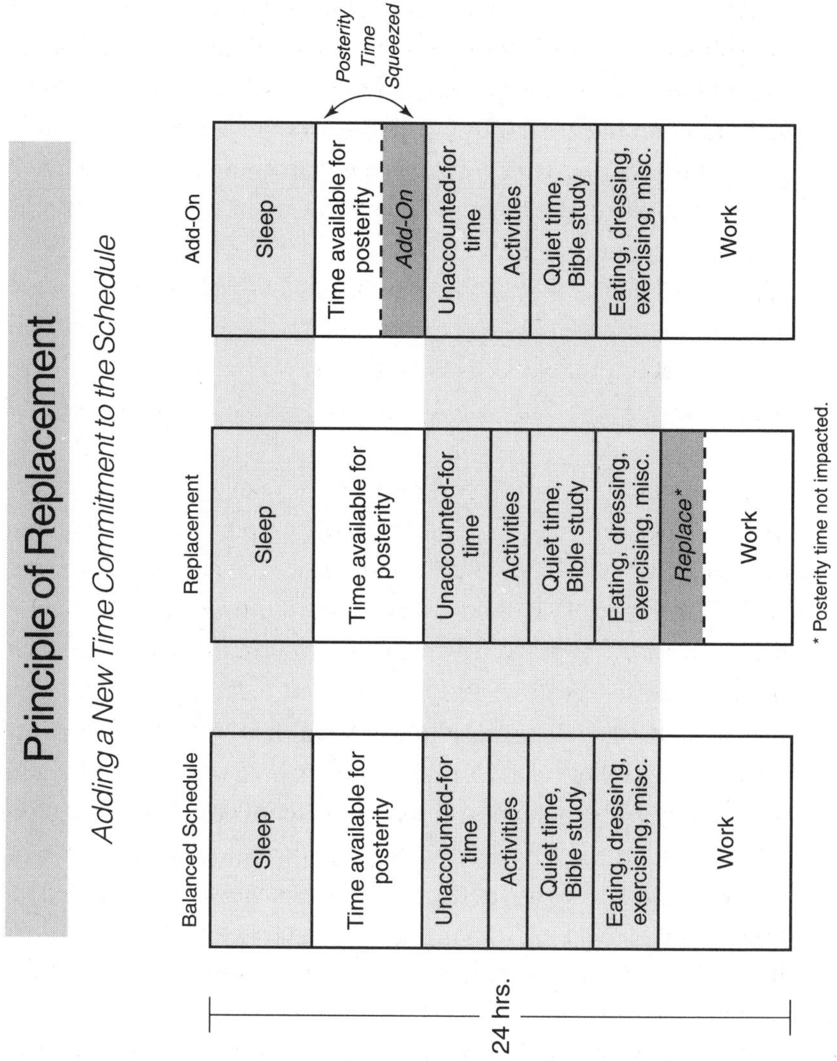

Principle of Replacement

Adding a New Time Commitment to the Schedule

Balanced Schedule

- Sleep
- Time available for posterity
- Unaccounted-for time
- Activities
- Quiet time, Bible study
- Eating, dressing, exercising, misc.
- Work

24 hrs.

Replacement

- Sleep
- Time available for posterity
- Unaccounted-for time
- Activities
- Quiet time, Bible study
- Eating, dressing, exercising, misc.
- *Replace** / Work

* Posterity time not impacted.

Add-On

- Sleep
- Time available for posterity / *Add-On*
- Unaccounted-for time
- Activities
- Quiet time, Bible study
- Eating, dressing, exercising, misc.
- Work

Posterity Time Squeezed

commitments to my schedule usually involves a trade-off between work and posterity time.

One obvious objection people might have is, "But I must work as much as I can because our family needs the money." *Aha!* That objection actually contains a key point. We need to make good financial decisions and budget our money prudently so we have the flexibility to replace work time with posterity time. Managing our finances is critical—not to have more money to spend or to be able to retire, but to buy time for our posterity.

Build a schedule that leaves you a margin of time for your posterity. Only say yes if it replaces something else that's already in your schedule.

Understanding this principle made it easy for me to say no when our church asked me to be an elder when the children were young. Because of the needs of the children and my work requirements at that time, the church work did not fit into my schedule. It could only be an add-on. In other words, to say yes to that commitment would have reduced the time margin I had built into my schedule, and that margin was for my posterity. However, as I got older and my children graduated from high school, I was able to say yes and allow time in my schedule to serve as an elder.

Unfortunately, too many of us do not say no. We simply add more and more to our schedules. What ends up getting replaced is the time we had for our posterity. My encouragement to you is to build a schedule that leaves a margin of time for your posterity. *Only say yes if the activity can replace something else that's already in your schedule that doesn't detract from your posterity time.*

Our Inability to Slow Down

The second obstacle that takes away from our posterity time is our inability to slow down. In today's world everything moves quickly and we're constantly striving to see if we can make it go even faster. If the computer lags when it's started up, we want a new computer. If the fast-food line takes more than two minutes, we get impatient and go to a different restaurant. *Progress* is the term we use to describe this increased speed and the ability to utilize every second to the maximum, but many times I wonder if speed really equals progress. Richard Swenson offered some intriguing comments in *Margin*:

> Progress has given us unprecedented affluence, education, technology and entertainment. We have comforts and conveniences other eras could only dream about. Yet somehow, we are not flourishing under the gifts of modernity as one would expect. We have ten times more material abundance than our ancestors yet we are not ten times more contented or fulfilled…Margin has been stolen away and progress was the thief. We must have room to breathe. We need freedom to think and permission to heal. Our relationships are being starved to death by velocity. No one has time to listen, let alone love. Our children lay wounded on the ground, run over by our high-speed good intentions.[5]

It seems to me that this frenetic pace is a real detriment to our ability to establish the building blocks of our posterity. Why? Because it leaves us no leisure time. Consider this statement by Gil Schwartz in a *Fortune* magazine article: "Before capitalism, the pace of work was relaxed. Our ancestors may not have been rich, but they had an abundance of leisure. When capitalism raised incomes it also took away the time."[6]

Similarly, Jeremy Rifkin, in his book *Time Wars,* commented, "According to a Harris Survey, the amount of leisure time enjoyed by the average American has decreased 37 percent since 1973. Progress was billed as leisure-permitting and time-gifting. The opposite has been true." He continued by stating, "The modern world of stream-lined transportation, instantaneous communication, and time-saving technologies was supposed to free us from the dictates of the clock and provide us with increased leisure. Instead there seems never to be enough time. Tangential or discretionary time, once a mainstay, an amenity of life, is now a luxury."[7]

James Dobson once watched people as he sat in an airport and later noted his observations in an article for the *Focus on the Family* newsletter:

> I saw busy, exhausted men and women who appeared to be hours behind schedule. Would it really create an international crisis if they pulled up a chair beside me and watched the world go by for a few minutes? I know! I know! Planes don't wait!
>
> What a price we pay for the speed at which we run! Already, the new year we greeted last January has dwindled to its twilight hours. It will soon recede into history. Most of us remember these last 12 months as a blur of activity. There was so much work to do. There were so many demands on our time. There was so much pressure.
>
> Meanwhile, what should have mattered most was often put on hold—or shortchanged—or ignored altogether. Millions of children received very little love and guidance this year from their busy parents. Husbands and wives passed like ships in the night. And our spiritual nature languished amidst overcrowded schedules and endless commitments. There must be a better way to approach the responsibilities of living…the enduring virtues of family, friendship and

our Christian faith. Overcommitted schedules and exhausting lifestyles undermine them all. That *could not* be God's will for us!...

As we approach the new year, will you join me in making a renewed effort to slow the pace of living?[8]

Our inability to slow down our pace was vividly illustrated to me when Julie and I joined another couple on a visit to the Biltmore House in Asheville, North Carolina. This house was built by the Vanderbilts of railroad-industry fame and fortune in the mid-1800s. What caught my attention as we went on a tour were the large eating rooms with adjoining sitting areas. Much emphasis was placed on mealtime in those days, and it wasn't uncommon for each meal to last two hours. So much of the space in the house was allocated to the dining rooms and breakfast areas because the family spent a lot of time there in conversation and dialogue—before, during, and after meals. It was during these conversations that values and training of the next generation took place.

What a contrast to the typical American family today—ours included. When the kids were younger, I would rush home from work in time to eat a quick bite with the family (a hurried, fifteen-minute meal) before Julie had to rush to a meeting and I had to take one of the boys to soccer practice. This scenario is replayed by many families night after night and weekend after weekend. We probably did not spend two hours a week together as a family around meals, let alone two hours at each meal. Dr. Patrick Malone commented:

> We have created a society in which we're living too close, too fast and with too much stress...It's largely a result of the decline of the traditional family, in which children lived in a home with two parents, the family ate meals together at regularly scheduled times and fathers interacted with their offspring...Families don't sit down at the dinner table together

anymore. A lot of families don't even have a regular dinner time because they might not all be there at the same time.[9]

As our society has become more urban and less agrarian, our pace has quickened and the demands on our time have increased. In the early part of the twentieth century, children spent much time with their parents in their workplace, whether in the shop or on the farm or in the kitchen—an arrangement that was useful for training and instruction. This scenario is much less true today. Children typically don't have the opportunity to go with their parents to their places of work. This means time is needed during other parts of the day for the training and instilling of values that, in the past, naturally happened in the course of the family's daily togetherness. Is it any wonder time replacement is needed?

Society's hectic pace is accelerated by kids' endless activities, technology, financial strain, commutes, geographic logistics, and so on. There is no shortage of demands for our time.

The changes in geographic logistics illustrate this nicely. In the smaller communities of the past, churches, schools, Bible studies, work, and Little League games didn't require the time commitment they do today in urban America. Rather than commuting to neighboring towns, you could walk to the ball field and school, usually in five or ten minutes. Although this situation still exists in smaller communities, it has become the exception rather than the norm as more and more people commute longer and longer distances to their jobs. Time is stolen by these long commutes, our pace is accelerated, and the quality of our lives suffers. Dr. Swenson summed it up when he wrote, "Chronic overloading also has a negative effect on our spiritual lives. We have less time for prayer and meditation, less energy for service and less interest in relationship."[10] To that I might add "less time to invest in our posterity!"

To redeem teaching time and cultivate relationships, Julie and I began to guard our evenings and especially our family's mealtimes. We did this by minimizing the number of things we said yes to, including meetings or groups that met in the evenings during the week. We were convinced that a relaxed mealtime together and the time after the meal were great opportunities to pass on values. We didn't answer the phone during meals (fortunately we didn't have smartphones to deal with, but I would like to think we would have turned them off). We used that time for conversations about the day's events, for reminding our boys about good table manners, and for helping them learn how to relate to and talk with adults. The after-meal time was a good time to wrestle and play games together. It was also a time when Julie and I could read stories to the boys. If the weather permitted, we also worked in the yard or did projects around the house together. Overall, while the children were young, we tried very hard only to do things that included them. This is why I didn't play golf for several years—it was something they could not yet enjoy. Now I enjoy playing golf again as the boys join me on the course.

I also recognize that many good activities—Bible study and sports, for example—can occur during the week. I know it's almost impossible to avoid a few nights where meals are eaten in the car or in a rush as we fly out the door to some activity. Still, we may be able to cut out a Bible study or an activity so we can spend more time with our children.

As a working dad who needed to travel for his job, I tried to make sure that when I did have to travel over a weekend I made up for it at a later time by taking an extra day off. I tried not to be gone on weekends at all, but it sometimes happened. I also tried not to be gone too many nights in a row.

The process of deliberately slowing the pace is unique to each family. The key is to be aware of the problem and take positive steps toward change. Otherwise a hectic pace is a killer of purposeful and strategic living; it shortchanges our posterity.

Our Inability to Turn Off Technology

A third obstacle that steals our time is technology. The options available to us continue to grow and compete for our time. Television used to be the main culprit and it was only available when we were at home. Now technology is always with us at our fingertips. We have all seen the couple or family eating out at a restaurant and each of them is glued to their own smartphones. Or children watching television in the car instead of engaging in conversation with their parents or siblings. We have missed so many opportunities right in front of us to connect with our posterity. And, as the saying goes, the days seem long but the years are so short and go by in a blink of an eye. Julie and I had much less technology to compete with when we were raising our boys, but we found that if we really focused on the priority of raising godly posterity, there was very little time for television. I found the following essay quite insightful and revealing:

The Twenty-third Channel

The TV set is my shepherd, my spiritual growth shall want. It maketh me to sit down and do nothing for His name's sake, because it requireth all my spare time. It keepeth me from doing my duty as a Christian, because it presenteth so many good shows that I must see.

It restoreth my knowledge of the things of the world, and keepeth me from the study of God's Word. It leadeth me in the paths of failing to attend the evening worship services, and doing nothing in the kingdom of God.

Yea, though I live to be a hundred, I shall keep on viewing my TV as long as it will work, for it is my closest companion. Its sounds and its picture, they comfort me. It presenteth entertainment before me, and keepeth me from doing important things with my family. It fills my head with ideas which differ from those set forth in the Word of God. Surely, no good thing will come of my life, because my TV offereth me no good time to do the will of God; thus I will dwell in spiritual poverty all the days of my life.[11]

I'm not suggesting that you throw out technology (is that even possible in today's world?), but my recommendation is that you turn your focus to training your children and passing on values. Don't let the culture around you do it. Sometimes when you watch television or movies together with your children, you can use them as a teaching tool.

Our Inability to Control Our Desire for Possessions

In many cases, the toys and gadgets we purchase consume our time instead of giving us more leisure time. "Paradoxical as it may seem, modern industrial society, in spite of an incredible proliferation of labor-saving devices, has not given people more time to devote to their all-important spiritual tasks; it has made it exceedingly difficult for anyone, except the most determined, to find any time whatever for these tasks," observed E.F. Schumacher. "In fact, I think…the amount of genuine leisure available in a society is generally in inverse proportion to the amount of labor-saving machinery it employs."[12]

We have more and more stuff to take care of, clean, repair, and look after. For example, we may buy a second home or even a third home and feel it's a good investment for our posterity, but if we end up spending more time taking care of the new home than we spend enjoying it with our posterity, it could be a detriment. It may be okay to have a boat as a means of creating family memories, but if your time is consumed with cleaning or repairing the boat and you don't spend time with your children as a result of it, the boat becomes a negative factor for your posterity. Or if the boat puts you under financial bondage so you have no flexibility to do anything but work to pay it off, it may be a negative.

The time we have to lay the foundation of social and spiritual capital goes by so fast that if we are not careful, then we will miss it. When children are young, they *want* to be around us and they will allow us to train them, but as they get older this changes. As they reach the teenage years the teachable moments decline.

A number of years ago, Jeff Davidson wrote what I consider a classic article for *Focus on the Family* magazine that captures the essence of this issue:

> At quarter of eight, as always, he is sitting across the breakfast table of his 17 winters, sipping and munching, palming back a sheaf of morning hair, an ear cocked for the mating call of the school-bus horn.
>
> And I miss him.
>
> Yet there he sits, still within my reach, intent on blading over each open space of toast with strawberry jam. He misses me not; his sapling mind is rooted in the unsentimental present. He is revving up for flight.
>
> Seven minutes to go before the end of breakfast, a hundred breakfasts to the end of childhood. This swiftly coming September, his place will be empty and unsticky, and he will be licking from his fingers the strawberry jam of independence. Like the generations before him, from the feet of Socrates to the backfield of Notre Dame, he will be a college man.
>
> Wait a minute. Please. Who says there's such a big hurry to launch his frail bark on the river of whatever? Where have all the breakfasts gone? The bed-time stories, the birthday cakes, the finger paints, the knee patches, the model planes, the goalie gloves and hiking boots, the facts of life, the SATs, the hanging gardens of disco?
>
> We have awakened together 6,000 times. Can't I save any of them for a sunless day? We have eaten 15,000 meals together; why can I remember only half a dozen? What has been the rush?
>
> I crystal-clearly remember the bubbly babble and the rhythmic creaking of the crib; and, after they lanced his infant finger, bearing the white bundle of him shrieking through the street, his mother pale at this first communion

with pain. I know we wrestled on the big country bed, and I am sure I heaved his wiry, giggling frame over and over and over onto a green mountain of hay—I remember the smell of fresh-cut grass and his hair shimmering in the mottled sunlight. But then I skip all the way to some black-night downpour in the Maine woods: he is laughing against the rain and spinning the front wheel of his bike so I can squint at a sodden map in the dim, spotted glow of its headlight. The next thing I know, we are posing triumphant on the peak of an Alp.

But what about the valleys? Where are the Tuesdays, the Februaries? When was 11 years old? Whatever happened to 1978? Did we let the rest of it speed away in homework assignments, the purchase of sneakers and vacant Sunday afternoons? Why didn't we take more trips to the moon?

We talked about chocolate ripple and subordinate clauses and the four-minute mile—but did we ever get around to love, honor, truth?

He does not hear me thrashing through these last-minute woods: he stirs his placid coffee and blithely leans the spoon face-down against the saucer.

And yet, if I could look into the present and stare it to a standstill, I would freeze his spoon in mid-coffee and hold this semiprecious moment sharp and clear forever. The breeze leafs gracefully through the open book. Something smells of cinnamon. His mother's arm is raised in an offer of bread, and a faucet drips. I try to keep this ordinary, heartbreaking Now from drifting cloudlike into Later. No one will move a muscle. None of this will ever come again.

A whole fugue of noises will be erased from the sound track of our house. Duet for muffled telephone conversation and slamming door. Concerto for hair dryer, open refrigerator and pre-dawn house key. What is the sound of no guitar strumming?

With the change of season, the markers that show he passed along this trail will fade: the scattered books, open to the last idea that lost his darting interest; the music stand at the crossroads of the living room; the randomly slung seven-layer cake of the week's assorted garments.

No more midnight parleys in that two-man's land between our bedrooms. Requests to determine how was school today will have to be put in writing. We will use the telephone for love and hurt and urgency, where once it was just for matters of lunch and dinner.

For him to see us, from autumn on, will require a decision, an act of the will—not just a friendly jostle in the common corridor of our lives. I wonder how much of me he will afford in his future.

This May Monday, I am still a little more equal than he, but already he patiently explains to me disk drives and computer terminals. How long until I am just a memory chip, programmed for Friday-night dinners?

He glances coolly at his watch, as if all it told was heartless time.

I put a warm reassuring arm around his shoulder. This is not our first rite of passage. We have been flight trainees together since that first nursery-school September, when he was dropped by stroller behind enemy lines. After all, we weathered summer camp and survived the first shave. This too may pass.

God knows I am happy for him. So crack the champagne and let him glide out to sea. Give him liberty or give him life. No matter what, I will never confess that I am a tiny bit jealous of all that youth and romance—that I hope now and again the brittle world will make him yearn for the pliable pleasures of home-cooked tenderness.

Go with lump-throated blessing. Take up your stick

and red bandanna and pocket calculator, and to thine own self be true. There will always be a fatted calf in the freezer.

But don't let this night be different from all other nights. Please borrow my razor and hang up no clothes. Sing loud, sweet stereo. Strew the neat spaces of our middle age with vibrant disorder.

We will mark off this countdown with little banners of trivial joy. Under the unseeing nose is where they were hidden the whole time. Don't you see, says the last clue, Monday morning is the treasure. Breakfast is a trip to the moon!

So let us savor this day our daily toast. Rejoice in the peal of knives on jam jars. Tell me, before it's too late, what you dreamed about last night or what you want to be when the world grows up.

The wind sits in the shoulder of his sail, and they are waiting for him. A rush-brush of teeth, a grab bag of books, and the door slams me into silence. I shuffle back to the still-life breakfast table. The foghorn of the school bus wails him to distant shores.

Bye. Thanks for the childhood. See you tonight.

Left at the corner, then straight ahead until you hit the world.[13]

Yes, it's only a short time until our children will only see us at their initiative, so we must redeem the time now, before it is too late. In the next chapter we will analyze our present vocation in light of the needs of our posterity.

◦ FOR FURTHER REFLECTION ◦

1. What are some ways you could invest your money to buy more time for your posterity?

2. What obstacles do you face that steal time from you?

3. In what ways do you struggle with the consequences of a hectic pace?

4. What specific steps could you take to reduce the pace in your life?

5. Are there activities that you should consider saying no to at this stage of your life? If so, are you willing to step away from those? Why or why not?

6. What are three things you can do this week to help your family unplug from technology and instead, use that time for investing in each other?

A New Understanding of Work

*Analyzing Our Careers in
Light of Our Posterity*

*They lived in a hurry. He gave them everything a father
could provide. She was all a mother could be. But the
children grew fast and far away and one day all that was left
was fifty years of memories for sale in THE ESTATE SALE.*

"ESTATE SALE" VIDEO, WHITE LION PICTOGRAPH PRODUCTIONS

*But Martha was distracted with much serving...And
Jesus answered and said to her, "Martha, Martha, you
are worried and troubled about many things. But
one thing is needed, and Mary has chosen that good
part, which will not be taken away from her."*

LUKE 10:40-42

When our boys were young, I walked into the house late from work one Thursday night. I could tell by the look on Julie's face she was not happy. My mind raced back through the prior two weeks. I had missed dinner the past three nights due to some projects at work, but I couldn't see how that would have caused her frustration. I had told her I would have some late days during that week, so she should have been expecting it. But as my eyes caught hers, she quickly began to explain how I always seemed to be at work, how it appeared that I was never home for dinner, and the children were, as she said, "growing up without me." I was incredulous, but as we sat down on the couch and began to talk, the reason for her frustration became clear.

Over the previous two weeks I had been gone at night, not only for work-related projects, but also for two functions at the church and for two men's basketball games. In addition, Julie and I had hosted a school-board committee meeting in our home one night and had a young couple over on another night to help them with their finances. Fewer than half of the past fourteen nights had been spent with our children. Since work was the culprit the last three nights, it caught the brunt of the blame. The issue, however, wasn't just work.

Balance is defined as "the ability to keep in equilibrium, to estimate the relative importance or value of something." Julie and I have found that it takes a constant effort to balance our lives and keep the pendulum from swinging wildly past center.

Look again at the circle on the Life-overview Balance Sheet in chapter 4, which illustrates the need to balance the components of family, work, church, world, government, and a relationship with God. It's easy to get out of balance in any of the areas by taking time away from one of the other areas. For example, we could spend so much time involved at church that we neglect our vocational work. Or we could spend so much time evangelizing the world that we neglect our families. Obviously, being out of balance in any area could make it extremely difficult to meet the challenge of balancing posterity and finances.

Though imbalance can occur in any area, I'm convinced that in our society the most common and greatest threat to a balanced life occurs because of the tension between family and work. In this chapter we'll take a look at why this tension exists, primarily from the work perspective, and offer some suggestions about how to deal with it.

Family and Work

The tension between family and work is great because they both require a large time commitment. Yet the Bible is clear about our responsibility in each of these areas. For example, Deuteronomy 6:6-8 states that I'm to teach my children as I sit in my house, as I walk by the way, and as I lie down and rise up. Sitting, walking, lying down, and rising up require a lot of time! In Proverbs 22:6, I'm told to "train up a child in the way he should go." And 1 Peter 3:7-9 tells me that husbands and wives are to live together in a harmonious and understanding way.

The Bible is also clear about our responsibility to provide for our families. The apostle Paul said if we do not provide for our families, we are "worse than an unbeliever" (1 Timothy 5:8), and if we do not work we should not eat (2 Thessalonians 3:10).

The issues related to our church, world, and government also require time, and they cannot be neglected in raising godly posterity (as will be discussed later); however, these components are typically less of a time drain than family and work.

Over the years, I've kept excerpts of articles that clearly point out this tension. This sampling shows the sense of loss when the components of work and family are out of balance:

> *Billy Graham,* evangelist: "The greatest mistake was taking too many speaking engagements and not spending enough time with my family."[1]

> *Jane Fonda,* actress: "The few things I regret in my life are... not having put enough time into mothering, wiving, taking care of the inner life."[2]

> *Pete Petit,* CEO/Chairman of the Board, MiMedx Group, Inc.: "I've always tried to convince myself that I've spent quality time with my kids rather than quantity time. Now that I'm 50, I realize I've probably been naive about that.

You have to realize that parenting is an art, not a science. All your children are different, and have different needs. I'm sure my children have missed some things because I've spent so much time here at work."[3]

Peter Lynch, author and former investment-fund manager: "My problem is, I operate in only two gears, overdrive and neutral, and it's all been overdrive since about 1982...I had to return from it [family ski trip] early and missed seeing my daughter in a race. I was in here at the office when the market was closed and the family was skiing and I said, 'What am I doing?'"[4]

Garth Brooks, country music star (commenting on his daughter): "She's already taught me the greatest lesson in life—that *nothing* is more important than family...I see that little girl and think...'You've been chasing stuff that means nothing, and you've been running away from *this...*' The one gift that I want to give this kid is the best gift that my dad and mom ever gave me—attention—to know that every time I looked up from that bench at any sporting event, no matter how far away it was, no matter if I was playing or not, they were there. I don't want to end up coming off a concert tour and hear my daughter say, 'Hey, I recognize you from your record albums. You're what's-his-name.'"[5]

Dan Stamp, chairman and founder of Priority Management Systems: "People often say, 'For now, I'll focus exclusively on my career, but in the future, I'll do more with my family.' But by the time the future comes, by the time the person is ready to be a real parent, he may find that it's too late. The kids are grown up—never to be 5 or 10 years old again. Once those years are missed, there's no going back."[6]

So how do we balance the components of work and family? The experience I've gained at Ronald Blue Trust tells me the key is to have a correct understanding of work and income. This principle is the focus of this chapter. Second, I need a plan for my family so I know what I'm trying to accomplish with them. That will be covered in the next chapter.

Some readers may be further along in life and have already discovered what the individuals quoted above discovered—that we should have balanced our lives a little more. If this is the case for you, let me encourage you that it's never too late to build posterity. Even if your children are grown and have children of their own, you can still spend time with them. You can try to help them avoid making the same mistakes you may have made, and you can encourage them with their own posterity.

If you are in the early years of child-rearing or in the throes of it, then I am excited you have chosen to learn more about the value of investing in your posterity. I know it is not easy, but trust me—you will not regret it!

Variable-time vs. Fixed-time Vocations

I'm convinced that we should earn our money by working hard, by doing our best at the vocation God has equipped us to do during our allotted time here on earth—while at the same time allowing appropriate amounts of time to be with our families.

Young individuals without children typically have more time available to work. Those who are married and have young children have less time available for work because of the time demands from their family. As children grow up and move out of the home, a person's available time to work is once again expanded.

When I began to work at Ronald Blue & Co. (now Ronald Blue Trust), I would often go to the office on Saturdays to study for the Certified Financial Planner™ exam. I took Julie with me, and she helped quiz me. I also used to take two-week business trips to the West Coast to see clients, sometimes taking Julie along so she could visit with her parents while I worked. However, as the children came along, we no longer had some of those luxuries.

Your allotted time to work will be a function of whether your vocation is what I call a variable-time job or a fixed-time job. In a variable-time job you do not record your time. These vocations are typically not eight-to-five types of jobs but rather work that has fluctuating hours. In my job, I'm not required to submit a timesheet, but I have certain performance standards that must be met. Some days I may work twelve hours; others are much shorter. Through it all, however, there is always more to do than can be done in a reasonable day, so the pressure to spend more time at work is always present. This dilemma is characteristic of a variable-time job. The salesperson could always make one more sale, the doctor could always see one more patient, and the teacher could always grade one more paper. More can *always* be done! The question is, "Where do we stop?"

Conversely, a fixed-time job neither requires nor expects much involvement beyond the time spent physically at work. A factory worker, bank teller, flight attendant, or nurse are some examples of fixed-time vocations.

At our firm we work primarily with individuals who fall into the variable-time professions—business owners, entrepreneurs, doctors, dentists—since the variable professions typically generate the most income. On the surface it seems that variable-time workers have it made. They have time *and* money for vacations.

In reality these individuals have a challenge in building posterity that fixed-time workers do not have. They have to constantly guard against overworking. Overworking is any situation where a person is spending hours on his or her vocation to the exclusion of other priority areas, such as family, church, and personal time. The fixed-income worker clocking in and out doesn't typically have the pressure to overwork. Most days, he or she puts in the scheduled time and goes home. However, on the surface what appears to be a positive of the variable-time job—the higher income—is in many cases a detriment to spending time with family and training up a godly posterity.

Business owners are a case in point. In most situations they are not only the visionaries of their businesses but also the primary decision makers. Though they usually have sufficient income to buy "freedom" by hiring others to do some of their work, they are typically hesitant to do so for fear of losing some control. They simply can't let go of the decision making, and, as a result, their time is strained. It's not their own. Cell phones have allowed them to always be on call and available for work. They may be away from the office physically, but mentally the office streams through their consciousness. As the business succeeds and generates more income, the opportunities to grow increase and their freedom is reduced even more. They may have more financial capital than ever, but unfortunately they are spending less time with their families.

If you are in one vocation and are considering switching to another, be careful to evaluate the impact of the change on your time.

The medical profession offers careers that are respected by most people. They typically generate significant income and appear to allow for a lot of discretionary time for workers to be with their families. However, doctors are on call at night and on weekends, an arrangement that can put significant challenges on spending time with family, especially in the early years of their practices.

What about salespersons? Their income is a function of their own efforts, and typically the more time they spend at their jobs, the more income they can make. And their companies usually impose sales quota pressures (or they do it themselves). They want to constantly sell more and more so they can make more and more.

Many jobs seem to have no boundaries on the time that can be spent working. Most vocations that tend to generate greater income also tend to exert the greatest pressure on the person's time. If not handled properly, this pressure can steal the time necessary to invest in the next generation. Careers that put the least amount of stress on the person's time tend to produce less income and can put more stress on the financial side.

One final comment about overworking. Many persons may overwork, not because of the money, but because their identities and self-images are tied to what they do. We must recognize that our self-image is a function of who we are *in Christ*. How we view ourselves should not depend on our jobs. We need to restrain our egos and realize that God "resists the proud" (1 Peter 5:5).

Regardless of your vocation, consider the following observations as you struggle to balance your work and your need for time margin for training your posterity.

1. Find a vocation you enjoy and are equipped for, and then live within the income it provides.

It's your responsibility to work hard and well at what God has called and equipped you to do (Colossians 3:23), realizing that the income you generate is no surprise to Him. He sovereignly ordains it through your employer or through the clients or sales He allows you to have in your business.

2. If you are in a fixed-time job that has limited income, don't think you would be better off in a vocation that paid more money.

It may be easier for you to raise godly posterity because of fewer time pressures than it would be for the person who has the variable-time job and greater income. Although less income may result in more financial pressures, we will see in the next chapter that lifestyle—not income—is often the reason for financial pressure. Therefore, control your lifestyle, live within your income, and be content in the vocation for which God has equipped you.

3. Be aware of the different time demands at your family's different stages.

The needs and time demands are the greatest when children are young. Those demands usually subside somewhat through the teenage years and into college.

Let's look at how this works out practically. If you're starting a business and you don't have children yet, project what your time commitments will be later in the business as you start a family. If the growth of the business reduces your time commitments, that's good. But if business growth will require more of your time exactly when your children need you, you may want the business to grow more slowly, hire a key assistant, or stay smaller longer. If you're in one career and are considering switching to another, be careful to evaluate the impact of the change on your time. Also evaluate where you are in the different stages of your family life. If your children are young, you may be better off waiting a few more years until they're teenagers to make the switch. Or if they are teenagers, you may want to wait until they graduate from high school.

A friend of mine illustrates this challenge. He works for a huge corporation with an abundance of career possibilities. He is newly married, and right now he travels three to four nights a week at least twice a month. He makes a good income, is building a good 401(k), and enjoys a lot of nice perks. I've cautioned him, however, that travel won't be so glamorous after his children are born. I've encouraged him to project his career path for the next two to five years to see how his time commitments may balance with a family. If balance doesn't look possible, it may be better for him to look for another vocation now *before* the income and perks of the business make it too difficult to change jobs. If he's not careful, he'll be too far up the career ladder to get off but not far up enough to have flexibility over his time.

I know this concept of slowly climbing up or even getting off the ladder of success is a difficult one. In such cases, I always try to remind my clients to keep the big picture in mind and ask themselves what really counts for eternity.

I must add a comment lest you think I'm leaving God out of this equation. What if God "calls" you to another vocation at what appears to be the wrong time? For example, when a new job would take you away from your children. Using 1 Corinthians 10:13 and 1 Thessalonians 5:24 as cornerstone passages, I'm convinced that God is faithful and will not call you to do something He won't also give you the ability to handle. In this case, He will give you the ability and energy to stay balanced. It's hard, however, to fathom God calling someone to a job that would dilute His ministry in people's (and children's) lives.

4. Don't be in a big hurry to retire and quit working. Extend your work horizon.

One of the biggest obstacles to keeping work in balance is the "hurry up and retire" mentality. In our business we've found that regardless of how much money people have, in most cases, they will continue to work.

Work is good, and it brings fulfillment (Genesis 2:5,15). We were created by God to work, and if we don't work we may be quite miserable, as this *Wall Street Journal* article by Jeff Tannenbaum illustrates:

> An attractive buyout offer popped up and Mr. Gray sold out, thinking he'd never work again. "It was the great American dream of retiring." Trouble is, Dan Gray was soon climbing the walls. He found little to do but mow his lawn and visit Dan Enterprises as a consultant whose advice was usually ignored. "All of my friends were off working," he recalls. "There was nobody to play with." Within a year and a half, Mr. Gray started another T-shirt maker, Advance Industries, Inc., which he still runs. He had learned a lesson: "People who build companies can't get used to just stopping. It

makes you crazy." In the lives of entrepreneurs, few periods are more stressful than that which Steven Berglas, a Boston psychotherapist, calls "harvesting time." Some business owners feel burned out in their jobs but hesitate to "harvest" because they have no idea of what to do next. Others sell, but grossly underestimate the personal adjustment problems they will face later even if they're rolling in money.[7]

You have your entire lifetime to work, and only twenty years to make the primary impact on your posterity. Therefore, *earn your income slowly.* Spread your earnings over a forty- to fifty-year period. You don't have to be a millionaire by the time you're forty, nor do you need to retire at fifty-five.

William Johnston of the Hudson Institute said, "Policymakers might want to encourage people to take more leisure earlier in life, then work longer later on or never really retire at all. Workers in their 30s or 40s could be granted sabbaticals to travel or raise children, drawing down some pension funds in exchange for working to age 70 or 75."[8] This plan seems like a great idea in light of the tension between family and work in the early years of one's life.

William Mattox, Jr., of the Family Research Council in Washington, D.C., commented:

> The brawnpower to brainpower shift makes increasingly possible a long-overdue reordering of work and family responsibilities over the life cycle. Curiously, American families currently devote greater hours to paid work during the stage in life when they are most apt to have childrearing responsibilities and fewer hours (if any at all) than during the twilight years of life (between ages 55 and 70) when they are least apt to have dependent care duties. This peculiar distribution of work and family responsibilities (which, it should be noted, has become even more pronounced in recent years due to rises in maternal employment and early retirement)

may have been justified in earlier days when young, strong backs were in greater demand than seasoned, sharp minds. But with recent economic shifts, along with the rise in average life expectancy, it no longer makes sense to order responsibilities in this way.[9]

One of the greatest causes of midlife crisis is that many people work so hard and go so fast they accomplish all their goals by the time they reach forty. Then they wonder, "What's next?" What's next is what they forgot. They forgot to spend time with their kids and spouse, and by then, in many cases, it's too late.

5. Only change vocations to better fulfill your purpose and maximize your time flexibility—not to make more money.

As Solomon said in Ecclesiastes, "He who loves silver will not be satisfied with silver; nor he who loves abundance, with increase. This also is vanity" (Ecclesiastes 5:10). A change in vocation will by necessity require a greater time commitment. You must invest time to learn the new job. This may be all right if the investment of additional time doesn't last too long and will result in more time, flexibility, and options later. However, many individuals change vocations in pursuit of more money, only to find that the cost to the family wasn't worth it. Also, making a job change often takes so much emotional energy that the additional income isn't worth the effort. We have only so much emotional energy. If we spend it all on job changes, we don't have any left to apply to raising our children.

This is not to say that no one should ever change vocations, but the costs need to be carefully weighed. It may be that you would be better off waiting and earning less income at your current job until your children are at an age where a job change wouldn't be so disruptive to them by taking you away from home more.

A friend of mine decided to change jobs. Although his motive wasn't more money, he underestimated the emotional cost. Not only were his financial pressures increased, but his time commitments increased as well. His wife needed to work because they were having trouble financially. This scenario wouldn't have been a significant problem if the children had been older, but they were young and needed mom and dad *then*—not in three to five years, when less time and energy was demanded by the new job.

I remember when I was teaching school right out of college and decided to change jobs. One of the teachers commented that I could make a change relatively easily at that point because I had no children, but that it would be harder if I were further down the vocational road. I didn't know what he meant then, but I do now. It would have been difficult to spend the time necessary to start my financial-planning career if I had had young children. In that case, I would have been better off staying in the secure, lower-paying teaching job, which for me had less emotional stress and time pressures. This doesn't discount following God's call about changing jobs. It's just that flexibility to meet other objectives needs to be a high consideration.

6. If you are in a variable-time job, set time parameters and do what you can do. Then trust God to do what you cannot do.

If you're a salesperson, specify a reasonable number of hours you're going to devote to your work. Set an amount that will allow you to provide for your family's needs and work hard during those hours. When those hours are up, stop working and spend time with your family.

Put time with family in your business calendar, just as you do your work appointments.

If you're in an unavoidable situation that requires you to spend a large block of time at work, try to make up for the overtime through extended and relaxed times with the family. As an example, I once had a tough week—I had three out-of-town trips in seven days, including four nights away from home. However, since I knew this was coming, I planned to take some intentional time with my family the week after the trip. I didn't schedule any early-morning meetings so I could have breakfast with the kids and a cup of coffee with Julie. When work does get out of balance, *make plans to bring it back into equilibrium.* Put time with family in your business calendar just as you do your work appointments. Develop the good discipline of planning to build margin by coming home early or going in late a couple days a week.

7. If you're in a career that is currently generating sufficient income, carefully evaluate additional time spent to earn more income, especially if your children are young.

If you have the opportunity in your vocation to opt for less income or to freeze your income and get more free time when the demands of your family are the greatest, consider doing it. Don't fall into the trap of thinking, *I'll work really hard now and make a lot of money, and then I'll spend time with my children later.* Remember, your children's first ten years are the most critical. If you're making enough income now, the extra time may be more valuable than the extra money.

An article in *Money* magazine illustrated this point quite nicely. The author wrote, "Once you've reached a certain level of comfort, the return on extra earnings begins to diminish—particularly if the extra work erodes your quality of life...You may be able to improve your life by reducing spending."[10] Here are some practical ways to implement this observation:

- Opt for a slower career path, and plan to work until you're age 70 or 75. In today's economic environment, many companies are looking for creative ways to compensate employees other than with salary increases. Some of the ways they're doing this are by offering flexible time schedules, alternative work schedules, and more vacation time and personal days. Don't hesitate to negotiate with your employer to benefit your family.

- If you're the boss, consider reducing your income so you can hire someone to free up some of your time. For example, a friend of mine didn't need the six-figure income he was making, so I suggested he use the extra income to hire some help. He did, and had more time with his children at a very strategic point in their development.

- As a trade-off, opt for more vacation time instead of salary increases. I know some companies allow employees to elect "vacation days" as part of their benefits package. The employee "buys" these days through reduced salary.

- Offer to work four-day weeks rather than five for 80 percent of your current salary.

- Offer to work six- or seven-hour days versus the traditional eight- to ten-hour days for less salary.

Of course, to successfully implement this observation, it's important to make good financial decisions and control your lifestyle so you don't need to earn more and more money.

Balance Is the Key

As noted clergyman Charles Deems once said, "All men must work, but no man should work beyond his physical and intellectual ability, nor beyond the hours which nature allots. No net result of good to the individual nor the race comes of any artificial prolonging of the day at either end. Work while it is day. When night comes, rest."[11]

Charles Spurgeon's comment on these words was right. No good comes from overworking, especially when the cost of the overwork is the family. An article entitled "Beyond Success" by Rob Phillips showed that even the secular mindset is starting to agree with the current thinking about balance:

> A young doctor cuts back his highly successful practice to spend more time with his wife and two children.
>
> An upward bound executive declines a transfer from the community where she's put down roots.
>
> A business owner allows his wife and children to reach him at any time by text or cell phone.
>
> A senior lawyer derives satisfaction from helping disadvantaged families through his church, and adjusts his calendar accordingly.
>
> The solution, they say, is to redefine success.[12]

Phillips went on to quote Dr. Steven Berglas, a Boston-area psychotherapist and psychologist, who said, "There is no more direct route to self-esteem than climbing the ladder and reaching for the top—when pursued from a balanced perspective...The entire materialism of the '80s has become politically incorrect. Now there is a window of opportunity to integrate meaning into the short-term self-interest that was characteristic of the last decade."[13]

As Christians, we should be at the forefront of this movement to balance life and integrate meaning into our lives. We must be prepared to handle the peer pressure of the world and even of some well-meaning Christians who will not understand us. They will wonder, "*Why* are you slowing down your climb up the ladder? Why didn't you take that job with more income? Why do you drive that old car and live in a smaller house?" The answer is that we look ahead to the end of our lives and realize we must make the tough decisions *now*.

In the next chapter we'll see that not only must we earn our money with balance, but we must also make good financial decisions so we have time to spend with our spouse and children.

⁓ For Further Reflection ⁓

1. List five vocations that would be considered variable-time jobs.

2. List five vocations that would be considered fixed-time occupations.

3. Do you agree that more income is typically generated by variable-time vocations? Why or why not?

4. Do you feel you are in a rush to retire? If so, would it be possible to slow down this rush? Would it cause you to lose your job? Do you have any creative options to accomplish slowing down?

5. Is it possible in today's society to balance work and family? If so, how?

Wanting It All

Four Major Financial Decisions that Affect Eternity

*Too many people spend money they
haven't earned to buy things they don't
need to impress people they don't like.*

WILL ROGERS

*The rich rules over the poor; and the
borrower becomes the lender's slave.*

PROVERBS 22:7 NASB

A gentleman went into the Apple store to buy a new iPhone. To pay
for the phone, he had to use three different credit cards. When
the cashier questioned, "Are you sure you can afford this?" the man
replied, "I can't afford not to have it!" He was a living example of Will
Rogers's famous statement. He was using money he didn't have to buy
something he didn't need to impress people, most of whom he didn't
even know.

It's easy to use our money to buy things. Consider this:

Mr. and Mrs. Thing are a very pleasant and successful couple. At least, that's the verdict of most people who tend to measure success with a "thingometer." When the "thingometer" is put to work in the life of Mr. and Mrs. Thing, the result is startling! There he is sitting down on a luxurious and very expensive thing, almost hidden by a large number of other things. Things to sit on, things to sit at, things to cook on, things to eat from, all shining and new. Things, things, things. Things to clean with and things to wash with and things to clean and things to wash. And things to amuse, and things to give pleasure and things to watch and things to play...

ANONYMOUS

You may be asking, "Is there something wrong with using money to buy things?" The answer is no, but the issue is bigger than buying what we want. The issue is spending and investing our money *strategically* to ensure that we have time to spend on investing in our posterity. The answer to the question, "How do you use your money to enhance your ability to balance your life?" is critical.

Four Major Financial Decisions That Affect Eternity

We're constantly bombarded with an assortment of things we're made to feel we can't live without. Most of us can't resist the pressure to buy. Before we know it, we have bought all of the latest technology, the newest vehicles, the nicest toys for our children, and the current fashions in clothes—and we wonder why our budget doesn't balance.

Carrie Teegardin described this in perfect clarity in her article "Load Too Heavy for Many" when she wrote,

> Some experts believe that the needs of a consumer economy have produced a new standard of living that people must work overtime to achieve. And it's a standard that Madison Avenue has been more than happy to reinforce.

> Some Americans still think they have to have a big house, two cars, state-of-the-art electronics and a nice vacation every year.
>
> They think they must work out three times a week at a nice health club, play golf once a week and send their kids to private school.[1]

We want to live like our parents live today when we are only a few years out of college, and we also want to "keep up with the Joneses." We've defined lifestyle by how we look, where we live, and what we drive. This problem is further compounded because consumers typically use debt to fund their desired lifestyles. Debt can be a shortcut to getting what we want now versus learning to be content in our circumstances.

Jason and Meghan Wanted It All

Jason and Meghan got married shortly after graduating from college. Jason graduated with a degree in business management and Meghan in nursing. They were excited when they both got jobs in the same medium-sized city in the Midwest. With two incomes and no significant drains on their cash flow, they moved into a two-bedroom apartment with great anticipation for a wonderful future. They enjoyed their time together as newlyweds, eating out a lot and traveling on the weekends. Jason even planned a surprise ski trip as a special Valentine gift to Meghan.

After a few months of apartment life, however, Jason and Meghan experienced some frustration with their living situation. They were disappointed that they didn't own a place they could fix up and decorate. They also wanted a yard for their dog and some space to entertain.

They called Katie, a friend in the real estate business, and told her they'd like to buy a house. In the meantime, Jason's five-year-old car, purchased when he was in college, gave him some problems, so he decided he might as well go ahead and replace it. He traded it in for a brand-new, moderately priced sports car. He thought it was a good deal, especially since both he and Meghan worked full-time and could handle the monthly payments with no strain on their budget. Conveniently, the car loan was stretched over five years to make the monthly payments lower.

While Jason was car shopping, Meghan spent time with Katie, looking at houses. She found a place she really loved but knew it was going to be a real financial stretch.

"You and Jason should receive significant salary increases over the next several years," Katie pointed out, "so the monthly payments will eventually become less of a strain on your budget."

Jason and Meghan thought it over and agreed with Katie. Even though the payments would be tough right now, they felt they both had potential in their jobs, and besides, it was a really great house. It was even nicer than the ones their parents lived in.

Jason and Meghan moved into their new house two days after their one-year apartment lease ended. As they placed their furnishings into the new home, they were astonished at how little room their furniture took up. They both agreed that they needed to buy more furniture. Over the next twelve months, the house became a project. Jason and Meghan spent a lot of time shopping for furniture and other items for the house. They spent time fixing up the yard, and soon the garage housed a new lawnmower as well as Jason's sports car.

In early June, they were surprised to learn that Meghan was pregnant—already two months along, with the baby due in January.

Although excited at first, Jason suddenly realized the financial reality. Not only would they have another mouth to feed, which would cause an increase in their living expenses, but what would they do if Meghan didn't go back to work? They had always figured they would have several years of two incomes to pay off some of their debts before children came along.

Jason and Meghan found themselves in a quandary. It was doubtful that Jason's income and future raises could support their current lifestyle with the decisions they had just made and the debt they had incurred. Only two solutions seemed possible. Either Jason would have to work harder and longer—potentially at two jobs—to try to make ends meet. This would leave him less time with Meghan and the new baby, taking away from building social and spiritual capital with the new family member. Or Meghan could go back to work, which would take away from her time with the baby and also incur childcare costs. This solution would also have a negative impact on the building of social and spiritual capital.

There was a third option, but it wasn't immediately obvious. Since Jason and Meghan wanted to have time with their new and growing family, they could reduce their lifestyle. As Carrie Teegardin said, "If Americans accept the standard of living the middle class enjoyed a decade ago, some say, they could spend less time at work."[2]

Easier said than done! Reducing one's lifestyle is incredibly difficult for those who have gotten used to living a certain way (and have used debt to fund that lifestyle). Lifestyle changes can also be embarrassing, since people often make friends with others who have similar lifestyles.

Before we look at some of the critical financial decisions we all face and their impact on our time, remember that these illustrations and principles don't apply only to young adults starting out. Some of our clients moved into their dream houses after their children were eight to twelve years old, only to discover that the additional debt they incurred put the same financial stress on them as it did on Jason and Meghan. If these critical decisions are mishandled at any point in life, the potential exists for stress between work and family.

I recall an individual who wanted to change vocations twelve years into his career. The new job was a better fit for his skill set, and he would have more time to spend with his family. He found, however, that this new job wouldn't pay enough to support his current lifestyle and debt load. He said the job "only paid $90,000"! His financial decisions had raised his expenses and his debt level so high that he had to make $125,000 to support them. Regardless of what the numbers are, the point is the same. Wise financial decisions at any age and salary level are *critical* in maximizing your *flexibility* to balance work and family.

The critical decisions Jason and Meghan faced also confront each of us—house, cars, lifestyle decisions, debt, and investment decisions. The impact of these decisions on our ability to balance family and work lead to valuable decision-making principles.

1. The Bigger House Decision

Buying a house is the most critical financial decision most of us will make. Not only does the price of the house dictate our largest debt obligation, but the bigger and more costly the house, the greater the other expenses—utilities, property taxes, insurance, furnishings, repairs, and maintenance.

*Never buy your first home
depending on both
of your incomes.*

There's tremendous pressure to buy too much house at two critical stages in our lives. The first occurs when we are just beginning our careers and families. Like Jason and Meghan, we're tempted to buy more house than we can afford because we think we'll be able to "earn" our way into it. In some cases, couples can do this without both spouses working, but the risk of depending upon future raises can still be too great. Throughout history, recessions have caused personal incomes to decline, which can lead to a foreclosure epidemic.

Any marginal time a couple may have to spend with their children during their formative years is often consumed by working to make money to pay for a house and all that goes with it. By the time they've increased their income to a high enough level to create some breathing room or margin in the budget, the kids are already halfway out the door—and past the age when parents have the most influence on them.

We recommend that young couples do several things. First and most important, *never buy your first home depending on both of your incomes.* Make sure you buy a home that will work into your budget on the income of only one spouse. Then when children come along you will have the flexibility for one parent to stay home. It's much easier to move up slowly in house size and price than it is to move into a smaller, less expensive house. It's okay to begin with a "starter home." Most young couples, influenced by media and peer pressure, want to skip the starter home and go straight to their HGTV dream house. (Isn't it interesting that America is the only country where starter homes exist? The term implies the buyers aren't going to stay there.)

Second, since many couples today are well educated and will both be in the workplace starting out, we recommend that one spouse's net income (after taxes) be saved. Simply act as if it isn't there and save it. Using only one salary and saving the other income will allow you to purchase a more affordable house today or a bigger house in the future as your salary increases and savings grow.

Waiting to purchase a home will also allow you to buy the same-size house with a greater down payment, thus reducing the subsequent payments. If one spouse's income will support payments on a $150,000 mortgage and you save $30,000, then you have two options. First, you could buy a bigger house and keep the $150,000 mortgage by applying the $30,000 to the down payment on a $180,000 house. Second, you could borrow only $120,000 by putting down $30,000 more on the same house. By borrowing less, you will reduce the monthly payments, giving you more discretionary income and thus more discretionary time.

Third, don't buy the lie that renting is always a bad choice. Often couples or individuals are better off to rent longer to save a greater down payment and reduce their mortgage payment, which maximizes their time and financial flexibility.

The second time in life when temptation comes for more house is about eight to fifteen years into a marriage. Several events converge during this time frame to create what often seems like an acute need for a different (and usually larger) house. First, all the children have usually been born. Not only are all the children on the scene, but they're growing and needing more room. Peer pressure to buy something nicer to "keep up with the Joneses" is greatest on mom and dad when they observe their friends trading up. After all, their family and work are in full swing and most of their friends have upgraded to nicer places, so they begin to feel they deserve a new place too. The husband is typically approaching middle age, and the big, new house can feed his ego in many cases. He feels he deserves his dream house after working so hard for all these years.

It's interesting that just when the family budget is usually beginning to get some breathing room (as a result of increasing salaries over the years and living in the older, less-expensive house) a couple decides to get right back under the pile. They buy the big house and stretch their finances all over again instead of sitting back and being content with what they have. Unfortunately, stretching the finances at this point can cause the rest of their children's formative years (the next eight to fifteen years) to be spent under financial pressure.

One of the best things a couple can do to balance work and family during their children's formative years is to live in the older, smaller house a few extra years. Instead of spending a greater percentage of their salaries on a new home, invest discretionary funds on family activities like vacations, ball games, or missions trips. Maybe the couple could opt for a smaller salary increase and more flex or vacation time to build family posterity.

I also recommend that couples avoid succumbing to the mirage principle. Most of the big houses that "the Joneses" are living in are not paid for. As a matter of fact, there's probably less equity in their homes than you have in your older, smaller home. They could be paying interest-only loans and not building any equity through mortgage reduction. If they have a hiccup in their income (such as a job loss, a pay cut, or an illness that causes short-term disability), then like a mirage, the whole thing disappears and they lose it all.

Many couples I know are "house poor." They work themselves to a frazzle to make the monthly payments and improve their house, and then they have no funds and time left to do anything else. The real travesty is that children don't care where they live. They just want mom and dad to be around and have some emotional energy and quality time to give them.

I'll never forget the comment of a friend's wife who lived in a beautiful 6500-square-foot home on five landscaped acres. "Russ," she said, "I enjoyed our 2500-square-foot home much more than this one. It was much easier to decorate, and the kids were much closer together. Here there's so much room we hardly see other. All the kids have their own rooms. It's a nice house…but it's not a home."

This isn't to say people should never buy a bigger house. Families do grow and need larger spaces, and homes can be great places for ministry outreaches. But choose the new home intelligently, counting the cost, maintaining life balance, and planning your finances prudently. Save for a new home versus defaulting to a much bigger mortgage and payment.

Here is an example of planning wisely. Let's assume I live in a $150,000 house with a $100,000 mortgage, and I can handle the payments easily on my current income. If, over an eight- to fifteen-year period, I'm able to save $50,000, then I could choose to buy a $200,000 house. I could put an additional $50,000 from savings into a new house and keep my monthly payments the same. Obviously, a more expensive house will have some additional costs, but the biggest outlay is the mortgage. The important issue in buying a larger home is maximizing your financial and time flexibility.

Second, only change houses if it will enhance the environment you want for your family (and not take away from it). Will the new house be a home? Or will it be just a house because you are never there?

Julie and I were able to blend these two recommendations in our own home purchase. We had an opportunity to purchase a property with some acreage when our boys were 13, 11, and 8. We were excited about the opportunity for them to have more space to run, play ball, play paintball, and so forth. However, during that time, I was also teaching at Promise Keepers about the importance of being out of debt. We had just recently paid off our current home, and I knew to move to this new property, I would have to continue to stay debt-free to not have added financial pressure. By applying the principle we're talking about, we made the decision to sell some other investments to raise cash and take all of our savings to add to the home equity in our current house to buy the different property. We were able to avoid additional stress on our finances and also create an environment that the kids have been able to enjoy over the years with their friends. As a matter of fact, even as Julie and I have moved into the empty-nest phase, children still come to our house to play soccer, play on the basketball court, and go out on the lake. I've never regretted implementing the principles to build up my savings to buy the new house rather than getting back under a monthly mortgage payment.

Parental Pressure

Many times the prior generation places subtle—and in some cases not so subtle—pressure to live a certain way. They might make comments such as "When are you going to get a new car (or a new house)?" or "Don't you think your children could use some name-brand clothes?" or "Why don't you go on vacation at that nice place on the beach?"

Often parents make these comments because they want their adult children to look a certain way. They don't want their children in a starter home because it doesn't reflect the right image to the parents' friends. They're embarrassed if their children and grandchildren are driving a ten-year-old car. A young couple needs to be aware of these motivations, and the parents of this young couple need to let them start out like they probably did.

If you are one of those parents, stop! Don't discourage the young couple from living in the smaller home and driving the older car a little longer. Don't make subtle comments about what you think your grandchildren need. Remember, the world they're raising your grandchildren in has more pressures than what you may have faced. School shootings, drug overdoses, and cyberbullying were not a part of parenting in previous generations. Today there is much for parents to navigate through that previous generations could never have imagined. Give your children some room and grace to raise their children as they make the necessary decisions that will instill spiritual and social capital in them.

James Dobson described it this way:

> The environment in which children are being raised has changed dramatically in the past few years, creating new anxieties for mothers and fathers. Unspeakable dangers haunt our schools and streets that were almost unheard of a generation ago. Yesterday's families didn't worry much about drive-by shootings, illegal drugs, sexual molesters and kidnappers. When I was a kid in the early 1950's, my folks were more concerned about a disease called polio than all sources of violence combined. As a 10-year-old, I moved freely around my home town. If I was a half-hour late coming home for dinner, the Dobson household was not seized by panic. But now the culture has changed! Now we worry about our kids playing in the front yard…Unfortunately, the risks to today's children are not limited to physical threats. Parents must also worry about the culture and how it impacts the hearts and minds of their precious kids…the struggle to protect their children from the culture goes far beyond junk food and celebrities pushing sneakers. It has become a

daunting task to shield the younger generation from "safe-sex" instruction in school, from profane and sacrilegious language in the neighborhood, from immorality and violence on television...[3]

This deterioration of society means your adult children's time with their children is potentially more critical than ever—and more difficult to come by. Encourage them to be in the fight. Don't pressure them, especially in the house and car area. Money and image are secondary to time with posterity.

Major purchases, such as a home and car, are not problems in themselves. However, when these two purchases require the use of excessive debt, multiple problems arise. The more debt a couple takes on, the less flexibility they have. It's been my observation that parents preoccupied with debt problems will often not invest adequate time and spiritual resources in their children, which threatens the children's spiritual capability and wisdom to manage the financial resources they will ultimately inherit. In other words, debt problems often cascade down multiple generations.

2. The New Car Decision

Jason and Meghan also made a few mistakes in their car-buying decision. First, they didn't pay cash. Instead they took out a five-year loan to get lower monthly payments, which ensured that they will probably owe more than the car is worth in a few years (known as being "upside down" on the car). The second mistake was buying a car that will be impractical for a growing family in another year or two. As a consequence, the sports car will necessitate buying another car. They could sell their "upside down" car and lose money on it, but then they might have to finance 110 percent of the cost of the new car. Buying new cars frequently will keep your finances on edge by always keeping cash flow tight.

*Pay cash for your cars if at all possible,
buy used instead of new cars, and plan
to drive your cars at least ten years.*

Simple car buying disciplines can pay big rewards. Pay cash for your cars if at all possible, buy used instead of new cars, and plan to drive your cars at least ten years. Fifty percent of all cars ten years old and older are still on the road. As the car ages, the costs of taxes and insurance decrease. Maintenance costs increase, but they are usually significantly less than the annual interest cost on a new-car loan. Buying used cars allow you to avoid the immediate depreciation that occurs in the first year or two of a car's life.

If you can't pay cash immediately, plan to drive your car ten years or longer and pay cash for your next car. How? If your current car payment is $400 per month and your car is paid off in five years, keep setting aside the payment amount per month in a savings account for the next five years. You will have accumulated $24,000 plus interest, and this should allow you to pay cash for the next car. The key to reversing the debt cycle is driving the older car longer. Julie and I have practiced this principle our entire lives and can say that we don't regret applying it over the years. At some point in the future we will need to upgrade, but we will pay cash for the cars and start the cycle over again.

Everyone dreams of buying a new car, but how long does that joy last? Driving older cars longer really does work to enhance financial freedom and give you more time options. The following letter, received in our office, illustrates what happens when this principle is put into practice:

> You stated that cars rarely appreciate in value and rather depreciate. Secondly, car purchases are really ego decisions,

not financial decisions. I wanted to share with you the story of my implementation of one of your financial strategies based upon these two points.

Returning to Atlanta, the lessons you taught were still fresh in my mind when I noticed that my next-door neighbor had a very old car parked in her driveway. It was the ugliest color of yellow that I had seen—faded canary like a banana!

I asked about it and discovered that it was bequeathed to my neighbor from her Great-aunt Mary in Chicago. It was a 1966 Plymouth Valiant with 106,000 original miles on it. No kidding—just driven to church on Sundays!

For whatever reason, a thought was planted in my mind that this was an opportunity to test my motives. Had I bought into the ego syndrome of auto consumption? Yes, I had. I had owned six sports cars in almost as many years, and most of them were bought new.

So I asked my wife what she thought about me selling my Saab and offering to buy my neighbor's car. Although she initially thought I was only kidding, my persistence conveyed my seriousness. She also had heard your presentation and was willing to support me in my decision. So I sold the Saab in a week, paid off the remaining loan, bought the Valiant, and put the savings in the bank.

The cost of the car? $300! It came complete with Aunt Mary's driving gloves and her hat in the rear window. So that I would always be aware of the temperature, the car also included a window thermometer from a Chicago funeral home that was attached to the driver's side window. (I guess she visited there often.)

Now I bet you're saying that was probably not a wise decision because of the potential repairs that I would have to make. Or there might be a lot of downtime and inconvenience. This is where I truly believe God was involved in orchestrating all of this. I have spent less than $350 in repairs in 2 years, and I can have her repaired at the local gas station or garage! I can do without those high-priced European service departments.

Was it a good decision? I believe it was. First, I broke the desire that I had for expensive cars. Second, I was freed from caring where I parked the car. Previously, I was always conscious of parking so that the doors would not be dented by others getting out of their cars. Third, I was totally debt free and was earning interest as opposed to paying it. I was a lender, not a borrower. Fourth, I needed that money a few months later in that I was accepted into the Harvard Business School and would need every dollar I could garner for tuition. Finally, it was fun driving Aunt Mary, the name my friends teasingly called the car. It was a conversation piece and a testimony of good stewardship.

Sure, it is a hassle being able to drive only 55 miles an hour. Aunt Mary (as we call the car now) just can't make it any faster. She is also quite hot in the summer because she doesn't have air conditioning, but that's okay. I just sweat a little bit in the afternoons. These are two small prices to pay for the rewards I have received.[5]

If you can pay cash for your car, it really doesn't matter what you drive as long as you aren't neglecting living a balanced life and your charitable giving doesn't suffer. If you can afford a BMW or Lexus, great. Just buy it based on the right principles.

Yes, it is possible to make good decisions regarding cars. It will not be easy, but the rewards are worth it.

3. Lifestyle Decisions

Another common mistake is developing expensive tastes, habits, and hobbies. Although luxury items can seem affordable early in a marriage when there are two incomes, later they can become tremendous drains on the budget. For example, Jason and Meghan's habits of eating out and frequently taking expensive vacations required a lot of money. Over time people can view these as entitlements and pay for them with a credit card. Instead, their attitude toward these lifestyle choices must change if their circumstances change. They should tell themselves, "If we can't pay cash or our income goes down, we won't do it."

Furnishing and decorating a home is also a lifestyle issue. Are you willing to wait to furnish the house until you have the cash? Or will you go into debt to get it decorated and fixed up as fast as you can?

Julie and I knew of a couple who had a beautiful old home decorated all in white. They only allowed their children to play in the basement because they didn't want them messing up the house. I wonder what kind of impact that will have on their posterity!

Another significant lifestyle choice is education. Many people are concerned about their children's education—and rightfully so. This concern, however, may lead to the pressure to send the children to private schools as well as to the finest colleges. On the surface this seems like good thinking; however, you must decide if your family can make those financial investments without losing posterity time. Perhaps saving that tuition money and homeschooling or being involved at a good public school is a wiser option. We must remember that we want our children to be *knowledgeable,* but being *wise* is more important. We, as parents, impart wisdom to our children, and that takes being present with them for a significant amount of time! Just as children don't care where they live, they don't care where they go to school as long as you are around and involved with their training.

I chose to have smaller raises and more vacation time when my children were young rather than the other way around. I knew I would have a lot of time to work while they were in college and beginning careers of their own. Also, because I embraced the principle of long-time horizons (which means not being in a hurry to retire), I wasn't under pressure to generate more income "now" to fund my retirement. Instead, we invested some of our "retirement money" in our children by using some of the funds for family vacations, trips to the ballpark, and paying off debt.

In this section we have looked at various lifestyle decisions about homes, cars, material possessions, and our children's education that can have a negative impact on a couple's ability to maximize their time and increase their margin. Before moving on, let's look at a principle that should make it easier to resist the urge to accumulate more and more things in order to keep up with and look like everybody else.

The Principle of Limited Sphere

When our boys were young, we typically traveled cross-country every summer on our way to Colorado or Kansas to visit extended family. In each small town we passed through, we observed the nice as well as the not-so-nice parts. It's never difficult to spot the home of the wealthiest people. We've observed that in each town one or two families appear to sit atop the socioeconomic ladder. They, and maybe even some around them, are undoubtedly impressed with their status and position in the community. But you and I don't even know them. Put that same home in a typical north Atlanta subdivision, for example, and it may be nothing special. And so it goes for every city. Hundreds of thousands of people all across America have grand homes, ranches, and buildings that nobody knows about. And most people will never know what you and I have either.

As I reflect on this concept, I conclude that the sphere of people who ever really know what we have materially is incredibly small. At most, there might be 75 to 100 people in my sphere who know what I have materially (what kind of car I drive, where my house is, what is in my house, what kind of clothes I wear, and so on). As a result, it doesn't make much sense to strap myself financially by buying things to impress such a small group.

No matter what a person has—a private jet, a mansion in the country, a lake home, a yacht—someone else always has more. On top of that, we all end up equal since we can't take anything with us when we die. King Solomon, one of the wealthiest men who ever lived, observed, "As he came from his mother's womb, naked shall he return, to go as he came; and he shall take nothing from his labor which he may carry away in his hand" (Ecclesiastes 5:15).

The only thing we leave is our mark on people and our posterity. The choice seems to be between investing our money in materialism to impress a limited sphere of people or investing our money in our posterity, who can change their world for the better and consequently impact an unlimited sphere. Think about it. If you train your children and they train theirs and they all impact others for Christ, the influence or sphere spreads. Consider the money you give to charitable causes and the worldwide sphere it can impact.

4. Investment Decisions

I've seen many cases where couples attempting to "make it big" took inordinate risks with their investments—only to lose their money. Often the motivation for the risk was good: to make a lot of money so they would have time and flexibility to spend with family. If the risky investments pay out, great. But what if the investment turns sour? I believe the risk is too great for most of us. Very rarely do people make large enough returns on their investments that they become financially independent. I've found that financial independence occurs by spending less than one makes over a long period of time, not from gaining big returns on investments.

I discourage taking undue risk with investment dollars until your children are at least eighteen. Instead, I encourage you to invest very conservatively to ensure that you don't lose your money. You can take all the risks you want when the children are older and no longer require as much financial stability. Besides, you will surely be wiser by then!

A Personal Example

Julie and I decided many years ago that our motivation for managing our finances was not to have more money so we could retire early or just to have more money. Instead, we agreed that our motivation would be to manage our finances correctly and wisely to increase our options and flexibility, to buy time, to reduce our pace of living, and to increase margin.

As stated earlier, we had an opportunity to change residences in the late '90s. We were able to do so (and still live there today), but we did not change our financial stress point relative to what our outflow was for housing. Anytime we've been tempted to take on additional debt to move into a place beyond our means, we reconsider how nice it is not to have the debt pressures that a new or larger home would bring. The rationalization that the kids would enjoy it and that if we wait until we can afford to buy it, they would be gone doesn't outweigh the debt pressures.

I think about the fact that because we don't have debt worries, we have discretionary income that enables us to go on family vacations and create special memories. I'm glad we're able to go out to eat or that I can buy special things for Julie without using credit. I'm glad that Julie could stay at home and pour emotional energy into our boys during their formative years. Staying in our home longer without a mortgage has also allowed us to make home improvements over the years that continue to bless us and our family. We expanded our back deck so that we have a larger outdoor area to entertain and enjoy God's creation, and we have renovated the basement to create a game room for our children and grandchildren so that we can continue to pour ourselves into our posterity.

Conclusion

If God blesses you financially and you can move without taking on more debt, then it would be fine to buy the bigger house. But I strongly recommend, and have a personal testimony to the fact, that you shouldn't do it before thinking through these four common financial mistakes. The same purchase decision principles apply to cars. When our kids were younger, we drove older cars (we were on the ten-year plan) and when the paint started to look bad and one had a dent, that was okay. Even though we could have used an SUV or a van as the kids got bigger, we didn't buy one until we could pay cash for it. We may have been crowded for awhile, but it was worth it because the kids really didn't care what they were riding in and we didn't add financial stress to our lives. Children aren't worse off for being a little crowded. As a matter of fact, we did realize we were crowded in our little Volkswagen before we traded it in, and the kids still missed that vehicle.

Finally, Julie and I are motivated to make good decisions financially because we realize that what we're buying is a rare commodity: *time*. We can either use our money to buy things that will not last (a bigger house, more toys, more stuff) or we can invest in our posterity, which will last. In the next chapters we'll look at how we can use the time we buy when we make good financial decisions.

⟶ FOR FURTHER REFLECTION ⟵

1. How does debt affect both work and family?

2. What lifestyle habits, if any, did you establish early in your marriage that have had an impact on your current financial situation?

3. Do you agree with the thoughts on education funding expressed in this chapter? Why or why not?

4. What pressures, if any, have you felt from your parents in the financial area? What pressures have you put on your grown children (if you have them)?

5. Do you have a financial plan? Is it helping you balance work and family? If not, what do you need to change?

Part 3

How to Use Your Money More Effectively

Train Up a Child

Building Our Posterity's Spiritual Capital

*I want to live one day over. With my children young
again. An ordinary day. I have so much to tell them.*

"Estate Sale" video, White Lion Pictograph Productions

*These words which I command you today shall be in your
heart; you shall teach them diligently to your children, and
shall talk of them when you sit in your house, when you
walk by the way, when you lie down, and when you rise up.*

Deuteronomy 6:6-7

We had just pulled into the garage when my first-born, Clark,
made another angry response to our third-born, Chad. As we
got out of the car I pulled Clark aside and I reminded him about how
anger does not please God (James 1:19) and how our words are to be
kind and gentle and edifying, not unwholesome and coarse (Colossians 4:6; Ephesians 4:29; 5:4). We talked about his need to ask God
to forgive him for the sin of anger (1 John 1:9) and to restore the relationship with his brother.

All the ideas in this book, and hundreds more, are part of the fabric of spiritual capital we want to weave into our children's lives. That's why we need time with them. We also have so much we need to model for them—especially in the spiritual capital area. In this chapter, we will look at the essential building blocks for a solid spiritual foundation for children. Remember, the spiritual foundation we are laying includes an understanding of biblical absolutes and truths, how to come to Christ, God's character and attributes, how to walk in faith and trust God, and biblical principles of money management, child-rearing, and marriage. Spiritual capital is using the absolute truths of God's Word to determine right from wrong and good from evil.

The four building blocks we'll look at—a global perspective; the training of trials and failures; the three biblical principles of giving, work, and church; and a heart for God—are by no means an exhaustive list. As a matter of fact, this is a rather short list that will deal with only a few areas that relate most directly to finances. I hope these will serve as an impetus for you to work on your spiritual foundation.

1. A Global Perspective

We must help our posterity see the world beyond this country. Early in our marriage, Julie and I had the opportunity to travel to Africa. That trip had a tremendous impact on our perspective of money and material things. We lived in an apartment at the time, and we had frequently bemoaned the fact that we didn't have a house. Also, since our budget was tight, we didn't have the luxury of going out to eat very often or buying the latest trends.

After two weeks in Africa, our apartment looked luxurious in comparison to the mud and, in many cases, *manure* huts in which many Africans lived. Just being able to eat what we wanted when we wanted with a *cold* glass of water from our refrigerator seemed great. Suddenly our older cars didn't seem to be such bad transportation after all. In Africa, we had seen the alternative—walking and riding donkeys. That trip gave us great perspective.

Our children need the same experience. They need to be exposed to more of the world God created, the different people in it, and the different situations in which these people live. That exposure should give them a greater appreciation of what they have and take their focus off money, possessions, and materialism. Having the name-brand clothes and the latest technology shouldn't seem quite so important to them.

You don't have to go to Africa to teach this perspective. A visit to the inner city of any major city in the United States should also change your kids' perspective on needs, wants, and desires. When the boys were young, Julie and I would help them go through their toys and clothes once a year to give to the less fortunate in our city. We would then spend a day delivering these items and seeing how others lived. We prayed God would use this exposure to help our boys take their focus off materialism and put it on Him and what was going on in His world.

If our children are to handle money correctly, they need to have a perspective beyond their needs, wants, and desires. They must understand generosity and realize the needs of others. *We must help them be stewards, not consumers.*

Pond water that doesn't move can become stale and stagnant and eventually polluted. A river, on the other hand, keeps moving. It remains fresh and clear as long as no trash is dumped in it. The same is true in our lives. If we share the financial capital we have and keep it moving, then we take the first step toward being good stewards. So we must not only expose our children to the needs around us, but also let them see us using our financial capital to meet those needs. They need to see us exercising stewardship, which Ron Blue defines as "the use of God-given resources to accomplish God-given goals."

To build a solid foundation of spiritual capital into our posterity, we must invest some of our current financial capital in experiences that give them a global perspective. We may have less financial capital at the end of our lives if we spend thousands of dollars to take our children to Africa or Russia, but the return on the spiritual capital will be worth it. Or what about having a missionary from Africa in your home during the next missions conference in your area? That may only cost you an additional meal or two.

A global view helps our children understand the differences between the temporal and eternal (2 Corinthians 4:18). If their focus is always on temporal needs and comfort rather than God's eternal perspective, they'll find it very difficult to handle any financial capital they may receive in a nonconsumptive way. Julie and I made this investment as soon as our children were old enough to gain a global perspective from the trip.

2. The Training of Trials and Failures

Trials and failures will also enhance our posterity's spiritual foundation. The Bible is very clear that challenges and difficulties are God's method of training, teaching, and growing us to maturity in Him. These verses depict this clearly:

> Count it all joy when you fall into various trials, knowing that the testing of your faith produces patience (James 1:2-3).
>
> In this you greatly rejoice, though now for a little while, if need be, you have been grieved by various trials, that the genuineness of your faith, being much more precious than gold that perishes, though it is tested by fire, may be found to praise, honor, and glory at the revelation of Jesus Christ (1 Peter 1:6-7).
>
> Now no chastening seems to be joyful for the present, but grievous; nevertheless, afterward it yields the peaceable fruit of righteousness to those who have been trained by it (Hebrews 12:11).

Despite these scriptural directives, most parents find it difficult to let their children experience trials. Often we overwork to earn more money so we can insulate them from difficulty. When they're young we buy them designer clothes so they can fit in and avoid the peer pressure and ridicule that might come if they look different. When they get older we make sure they have the latest technology so they are popular. We buy video games, designer clothes, and state-of-the-art toys. We spend our money—many times using debt—to help our posterity have it easy, comfortable, and pleasurable.

Think about the meaning of each of those words. *Ease* is defined as "freedom from labor, exertion, pain, annoyance; freedom from difficulty in great labor." Do we let our children struggle a little, or do we make life too easy for them? Do we drive them where they want to go on demand, clean their rooms when they forget, buy a riding lawnmower when the old one gets a little hard to push, or excuse them from taking out the garbage because they don't feel like doing it?

The definition of *comfort* is "to satisfy bodily wants and to free from all cares and anxieties." Do we teach our children to make do with what they have or do we quickly replace or fix the problem to free them from any anxiety? Do we let them drop out of a sport if they don't like it or refuse to try something new because they're afraid?

If our children have everything they want, how can they learn to be dependent on God?

The definition of *pleasure* is "doing what one wants; to experience good and delight as opposed to pain." Does my world revolve around my children? Do I always allow them to have their way, or do they have to learn to adapt to others around them? Are there times they need to be flexible and can't do all they want? Do we teach our children to be still and quiet in church or the doctor's office? Do we take them with us shopping or to visit a friend or do we get a babysitter so we don't have to train them to adapt and fit into our schedule? We need to be careful not to allow our children to be "lovers of pleasure rather than lovers of God" (2 Timothy 3:4).

If our children have everything they want, how can they learn to be dependent on God? As a matter of fact, ease may blind them to their need for God. In Daniel 4:4 (NASB) we read that Nebuchadnezzar "was at ease in my house and flourishing in my palace." He experienced comfort and pleasure. But it led to a pride and independence that caused him to forget God. In Amos 6:1 we read, "Woe to you who are at ease in Zion, and trust in Mount Samaria."

Of course parents want to make life easier for their children. On the surface, that's a normal, positive desire. However, overworking to buy things to make life easier for children can have a negative impact. As a matter of fact, making our children's lives easy and comfortable can make them complacent and lessen the likelihood of their being great for God.

J.K. Gresset said, "God prepares great men for great tasks by great trials."[1] A.W. Tozer said, "It is doubtful whether God can bless a man greatly until he has hurt him deeply."[2] Could we be crippling our children with the very things we are trying to do for them? We should be pursuing character and not comfort in our posterity. I agree with Randy Alcorn's sentiments:

> It is one thing to provide for our children, but quite another to smother them in things until they turn into self-indulgent materialists. An alarming number of children from Christian homes develop a basic identity as consumers rather than disciples. They grow up endlessly grasping for dolls, robots, plastic ponies, and everything else a production-oriented society can offer. Children raised in such an atmosphere—and that now includes most children in the United States—are often afflicted with the disease David McKenna calls *affluenza*. Affluenza is a strange malady that affects the children of well-to-do parents. Though having everything money can buy, the

children show all of the symptoms of abject poverty—depression, anxiety, loss of meaning, and despair for the future. Affluenza accounts for an escape into alcohol, drugs, shoplifting, and suicide among children of the wealthy. It is most often found where parents are absent from the home and try to buy their children's love.[3]

Scripture is very clear that one of the greatest detriments to following God is independence. Our material possessions and money may make us less dependent on God. In giving our children everything money can buy, we may cause them to lose a potentially close relationship with God. R.C. Sproul, the founder of Ligonier Ministries and a noted Bible scholar, wrote:

> Scripture tells us again and again that tribulation is a means by which we are purified and driven to a deeper dependence upon God. There is a long-range benefit to us that we would presumably lose were it not for the pain we are called to endure for a season. This is what Paul is teaching in Romans 8:18. Conversely, pleasure can be a narcotic and seductive; the more we enjoy it and the more we experience it, the less we see our dependence upon God's mercy and forgiveness. Pleasure can be not so much an angel in disguise as a devil in disguise to lead us into ultimate ruin. That's why we must be extremely careful, practically speaking, in pursuing too much pleasure lest we lose sight of our ultimate need for the mercy of God.[4]

Maybe this realization will make it easier to slow down and balance life rather than be in a hurry to accumulate wealth. I hope you are as challenged as I am to be careful how I use my money in the lives of my children. After all, "he who loves pleasure will be a poor man" (Proverbs 21:17).

Therefore, if you struggle financially, take heart, for you may be more prosperous than you think. You may find it easier to help your children learn to be dependent on God than the person who has a lot of income and discretionary money. If you do have a lot of money, realize the challenge you have to use your money wisely.

3. Three Biblical Principles: Giving, Work, and Church

Another key to developing spiritual capital in our children is to help them have a biblical basis for various life issues. They need to see life through the grid of God's Word. Although myriad issues are discussed in Scripture (including relationships, leadership, investments, marriage), three relate specifically to our topic: giving, work, and church.

Our children need to understand the principle of *giving* in addition to saving and spending. We tried to implement this in our children's lives at a very early age by setting up three banks. One bank is for spending, one is for saving, and one is for giving. Their allowance had to be put in all three banks. We wanted them to understand that all they have comes from God, and some monies must be given to acknowledge His ownership. Many of the financial problems we face today in this country, as evidenced by the debt load of most families, are because we are a society of greedy consumers rather than generous givers. Our children should learn to share all they have—including time and resources.

Children also must understand that God commands us to *work,* and that if we do not work, we do not generate the income necessary to provide for ourselves and our families. However, as parents, we have to model balance in our work life so our children understand that work isn't more important to us than they are, or more important than time with God. We will discuss this principle in greater detail later.

Finally, our work life should be kept in balance so we have time to focus on the *church* and the *world.* As discussed in chapter 6, balancing work and family is not enough. Part of that balance includes attending church and being involved in evangelism and discipleship. We must manage our finances correctly to have time to obey God's commands as well as model church and community involvement for our children. There is no better way children can learn these important values than to see them modeled by their parents.

How you are involved in the church and the world may look different depending on how old your kids are. Before Julie and I had children, we were very active in our church, leading a Sunday school class and discipleship groups. After we had children, we discipled couples in our home and cut down on the number of formal meetings and committees we participated in. With children prone to ear infections, we had to drop out of the Sunday school program and do Sunday school-type activities at home. As the children grew older, we were able to get more involved again.

What's important is that our children see us actively involved in some way in God's plan for the world: "Go therefore and make disciples of all the nations, baptizing them in the name of the Father and of the Son and of the Holy Spirit, teaching them to observe all things that I have commanded you; and lo, I am with you always, even to the end of the age" (Matthew 28:19-20). To do this we must keep our finances in order so we have time to focus on these areas in addition to our families. Our financial capital should also be used to create an environment that promotes and enhances spiritual capital. Therefore, you might choose to invest money in attending Christian family camps or short-term missions projects that encourage spiritual development. This trip may cost more than other vacations, but it may be worth it.

And if you don't have margin for these activities, don't feel that it's a detriment to your children, for most spiritual values are taught by parents spending time with their children.

4. A Heart for God

Helping our children learn to have hearts for God is another way of building spiritual capital. Let me suggest two ways of doing this. First, they should observe a calling in our lives that is bigger than what we're doing vocationally. They should see that our lives are purposeful and focused on following God's plan for us. They should witness that we go to work not just for the sake of working, but rather to accomplish God's bigger purpose for us.

I sense in my own life that this concept of posterity and prosperity is the message God has given me to share with the world. Therefore, as I travel, speak, and write, I explain to our boys what I am doing and why I am doing it. I pray that this wholehearted devotion to a purpose inspired by God will awaken imitation in them.

In chapter 7, I shared Billy Graham's statement in which he said he spent more time than he would have liked away from family. His son, Franklin, rebelled for a time, but eventually embraced Christ and His call on his life. It seems that Billy Graham's wholehearted devotion to God's calling eventually had a positive impact on his son.

Even in our fast-paced society, there is no "drive-through window" for knowing God. It requires purposeful meditation.

Second, our children need to see us praying, studying our Bible, having a daily quiet time, and talking about God in every aspect of our lives. During one of the presidential elections, we sat around the table after dinner and discussed how God sovereignly controls kings and rulers and that we could trust Him regardless of the election outcome. This discussion helped our children see that God is relevant in all aspects of life.

As our children see the relevancy of God in our lives, we pray they will begin to turn their hearts toward God and His way. It is difficult to teach our children to have a heart for God if we are always rushing off to work and never having time to discuss spiritual issues with them. We also can't teach them if we don't have a growing relationship with God ourselves. Even in our fast-paced society, there is no drive-through window for knowing God. It requires purposeful meditation. J.I. Packer, in his classic book *Knowing God*, wrote,

> Meditation is the activity of calling to mind, thinking over, dwelling on, and applying to oneself the various things that one knows about the works, ways, purposes, and promises of God. It is an activity of holy thought, consciously performed in the presence of God, under the eye of God, by the help of God, as a means of communion with God. Its purpose is to clear one's mental and spiritual vision of God and to let His truth make its full and proper impact on one's mind and heart. It is a matter of talking to oneself about God and oneself; it is, indeed, often a matter of arguing with oneself, reasoning oneself out of moods of doubt and unbelief into a clear apprehension of God's power and grace.[5]

We can't meditate without time! We must buy time and margin to be able to pray, study, meditate, and read in order to have something to pass on to our posterity. We need to be on guard against hurry and a too fast pace that can destroy these disciplines and render us empty, with no heart for God and nothing to share with our children.

There are countless other truths we must teach in order to build a spiritual foundation in our children, including absolutes vs. situational ethics, how to pray, faith, discipline, the fruit of the Spirit, and the importance of worship (Hebrews 10:24-25). All of these, however, just reinforce this point: We must balance work and family in order to have time to focus emotional energy on teaching these spiritual topics. How you go about building these ideas into your posterity is up to you, but I hope you're convinced now that money and the pursuit of it can, in many cases, hurt this effort. Spiritual training must be caught *and* taught.

⁓ FOR FURTHER REFLECTION ⁓

1. What steps are you taking to build the spiritual foundation of your children?

2. What are some additional spiritual truths you believe your children should learn?

3. In what ways could you invest your money to enhance this area?

4. Do you have a calling that is bigger than what you do every day that you should model for your child? How can you do this?

5. What are your written goals for your children in these areas—spiritual, intellectual, physical, and social?

6. Are you spending time with God to grow spiritually so you have spiritual values and principles to pass on to your children?

9

A Good Name Is Better Than Riches

Building Our Posterity's Social Capital

Good character is more to be praised than outstanding talent. Most talents are, to some extent, a gift. Good character, by contrast, is not given to us. We have to build it piece by piece—by thought, choice, courage, and determination.

JOHN LUTHER

You can't leave character in a trust account. You can't write your values into the will. You can't bank traits like courage, honesty, and compassion in a safe-deposit box. What we need is a plan—a long-term strategy to convey our convictions to the next generation.

TIM KIMMEL

A good name is to be chosen rather than great riches, loving favor rather than silver and gold.

PROVERBS 22:1

The quotes above by John Luther and Tim Kimmel are quite intriguing. They both clearly state that money does not buy character. On the contrary, they explain that character is developed by the strategic investment of time over a long period. No shortcuts and no amount of money can reverse this principle. *Character development simply takes time.*

Many parents live their lives in a hurry, amassing plenty of financial capital only to realize too late that those to whom they would leave their money have little or no character. The truth of this principle was never more evident than in the lives of a couple Julie and I knew.

Roger and Linda lived in a nice subdivision in an affluent section of town with their son and daughter. Roger held a significant management position with a prestigious manufacturing firm, and Linda had been with a local accounting firm for fifteen years. She enjoyed the interaction with the other adults, and her income enabled them to enjoy the finest vacations and to frequently buy nice new cars. They could also afford a nanny to watch the children when they were young.

The children were attractive and always had the best clothes and now, as teenagers, the latest technology and nicest cars. They did well in school and excelled in athletics. That's why what happened on an October night came as such a shock to Roger and Linda, as well as to the entire community.

The two children—ages eighteen and sixteen—along with two of their friends attempted to steal a new car from the local Cadillac dealership. In the chase that followed, they destroyed three cars as well as the one they were driving. All four children were injured and spent varying amounts of time in the hospital.

In this case, society was affected negatively (by personal injury and destruction) because these children were lacking social capital. The parents had given them countless things, but not the character needed to navigate society in a healthy manner. As the children served time in juvenile detention centers, it was too late to start the building process. Character development must begin at birth and continue into the teen years. Roger and Linda learned the hard way that the time they spent earning their money should have been balanced with spending more time with their children—time not only to train them but also to look for warning signs of lack of character.

The dilemma Roger and Linda experienced is the paradox that confronts each of us: We put our best time and emotional energy into making money only to realize the things that are really important (character qualities) cannot be bought with money.

What are some of the critical character (social capital) building blocks that our posterity needs to be effective, positive, productive members of society? The list includes a positive work ethic, responsibility, manners, sacrifice, stewardship, teachability, accountability, loyalty, integrity, learning trade-offs, honesty, discipline, ability to interact with adults, endurance, courage, morality, humility, and self-worth. Although one can have good social capital without spiritual capital, it seems that the long-term motivation for social capital flows from spiritual capital or biblical principles.

Many good books and other resources are available on how to train children and how to instill these character qualities into them. I encourage you to seek these resources, particularly those by Focus on the Family, Tim Elmore, and John Rosemond. The purpose of this chapter is to look at the impact finances can have on parents' abilities to inculcate these qualities into their posterity.

A Positive Work Ethic

A positive work ethic is an essential component to develop in your posterity. *Work ethic* can be defined as "the undertaking of the duty and obligation to exert physical and emotional energy in the person for a purpose." A positive work ethic is understanding the need to toil or labor—to work—to exercise positive influence in an environment to accomplish a task or goal. A work ethic contrasts with leisure, which is not involved in toil or labor but rather to be at ease. Laziness is adverse to labor.

Learning to work heartily is essential for at least two reasons. First, work embellishes responsibility, discipline, endurance, sacrifice, and accountability. Although these qualities may be taught without working, they cannot be taught as effectively. Second, since work (employment or effort that is productive and has a positive impact on society) is God's idea, children will experience fulfillment as they learn to work. In other words, work is the alternative to slothfulness. The former will enhance a good self-worth and fulfillment; the latter will destroy them.

The first step in building this component into our posterity is to teach them *God's view of work.* They must be taught to view work as good (Genesis 2), as a gift from God (Ecclesiastes 5:18-19), and as an activity that God commands (2 Thessalonians 3:10). Unfortunately, the society we live in views work as a curse—something to be avoided. That's why retirement is at the forefront of most people's thinking. They think the faster they can quit working, the better.

Unfortunately, many of us communicate "work is awful" to our children. We complain each morning as we leave for work about having to go to work, and our children hear us complaining at dinner about how bad work is. This modeling is why it's so important to enjoy what we do and manifest the truth of Colossians 3:23 in our lives. We must do our work heartily as though we are doing it for the Lord.

A second component in teaching a positive work ethic is to *model it* for our children. In other words, I need to be working. This intersection is where the tie-in with money and how one earns it becomes quite interesting. What if at age twenty-eight your financial ship came in and you inherited five million dollars? What would you do? Would your first thought be to quit working? After all, that would give you a lot more time to spend with your children and train them, right? Partially. You would have more time to train them in some areas, but you can't teach them the *value of work* if you're not working yourself. Also, if you're not working, how will you teach them about responsibility, punctuality, discipline, "stick-to-it-iveness," perseverance, and courage? These characteristics are all part of the work ethic package.

Why be in a hurry to make a lot of money only to quit working or buy a lot of indulgences and accesories, a second home, or more technology when quitting work or buying these things could make it more difficult to train your posterity in some of these essential character areas? I don't want to imply that you can't create an environment to teach your children some of these essential character traits if you're financially independent. However, it does appear that God, in His infinite wisdom, does accomplish a lot more through our working than if He just provided us with money. (One caution: If you don't keep balance in your work—if you constantly overwork—you will model that work is more important than family or church.)

If we let our children work,
they gain a sense of
accomplishment and teamwork.

Many years ago I met with a man whose investment income was sufficient to meet his needs for his family without working. His children were in their early teens. I was surprised to see him building his own house as well as getting involved in another business. When I asked why he was going to all this effort, he explained that it was so he could train his children how to work.

The bottom line is that you don't need to overwork to make money so you can quit working. Likewise, overworking to have more possessions can make it tougher for you to build some essential character traits into your children. If you have a lot of wealth, you may need to live as if you don't, at least in your children's formative years. It may be better for them to see you mowing the grass, painting the house, and fixing the faucet than always seeing you hire someone else to do it just because you can afford to. This is especially true when you work away from home, which limits the opportunities your children have to observe you working.

Finally, to teach our posterity a good work ethic, we must *let them work*. These days, we overwork to earn extra money for lawn and cleaning services while our teenage sons and daughters play video games or chat on social media. We overwork to buy things for our children rather than let them work and earn the money to buy the things themselves. If we let our children work, they gain a sense of accomplishment and teamwork. Self-worth is enhanced when children do things for themselves and are productive.

It's much easier for me to take out the garbage, empty the dishwasher, run the vacuum, and feed the dog than teach my sons how to do it. I can do it faster and without any problems, while the kids may break a dish or forget the dog or miss half the carpet. But how else are they going to learn? I remember the weeping and gnashing of teeth when I explained to my two oldest sons that they had certain responsibilities and chores around the house—all without financial incentive! It wasn't fair, they said. When I explained that other things could be done, such as cleaning windows or vacuuming the basement, to earn various amounts of money, they immediately complained that the pay was too low. But I knew I needed to teach them to work and also teach them the value of money. If I made money too easy to come by at home, they would be in for a rude awakening in the real-world job market.

There are an infinite number of ways to let your children work. Those options will change based on the ages of your children and your situation. What they do in the way of work isn't as important as that they do *something*. They should learn to finish what they start—to stick with it and see a project through to the end.

Once again, it's interesting to note that it may be easier to let my children work if I don't have a lot of money. The issue of housecleaning or lawn mowing will be settled. The children will have to do it because I can't afford to hire it out. I may not be as inclined to buy everything for them. They may have to sacrifice and work for some of the extra things rather than expect me to provide them.

Individuals who have a lot of discretionary income need to guard against setting up their children for a lifetime of disappointment. Lavishing them with gifts and requiring little work from them may not only diminish the children's work ethic, but also create lifestyle expectations that are hard to attain when they're adults.

There are times when money shouldn't be used to embellish some positives in the family. As we discussed earlier, money invested to buy time at different stages of your children's lives may enhance your training opportunities. Also, extra money to buy a lake home or take nice vacations together as a family may be a great investment. The money, however, isn't essential. It could be that camping out at the lake rather than owning a lake home or taking a creative, inexpensive vacation rather than an expensive one may be more effective.

Be careful not to fall into the trap of thinking that money (and lots of it) is what's important in life. It may be even more difficult to build the foundation of social capital into our children if we have a lot of money than if we don't. Consider these comments by Randy Alcorn:

> When we mistake the giving of material things for the sharing of grace, we do a great disservice to our children. A child who grows up getting most of what he wants has a predictable future. Unless he learns to overcome his upbringing, he will misuse credit, default on his debts, and be a poor worker. He will function as an irresponsible member of his family, church, and society. He will be quick to blame others, to pout about his misfortunes, and to believe that his family, church, country, and employer—if he has one—owe him. Having counseled numerous such adults, I believe many of them are this way because their parents, sincere but misguided, led them down that very path.[1]

An interesting question to ask might be this: "Is the inability to indulge our children really a negative given our desire to build spiritual and social capital into them?"

The "I Don't Want My Kids to Have It as Tough as I Did" Syndrome

Parents from the Baby Boomer generation often want their children and grandchildren to "have it better" than they did. I can't recount the number of times I have heard people say, "I just don't want my kids to go through what I went through," or "I want to give them what I didn't have," but this kind of thinking can hinder the development of social capital in our children.

> *The things we're buying [our children] make it more difficult (if not impossible) for them to develop the character traits they need.*

Typically the motivation behind these statements translates into an effort to make a lot of money to protect the children and give them things the parents didn't have while growing up. "What's wrong with that?" you ask. Well, did you learn and develop the character you have by getting everything you wanted and not having to do without some things? This attitude of not wanting our kids to have it like we did often leads us to overwork. Consequently, it detracts from the development of positive character qualities in our posterity.

Generations that grew up in the thirties, forties, and fifties *had* to work hard growing up, adapt to not getting everything they wanted, learn to wait (delayed gratification), and understand there are trade-offs in life. As a result, those generations became the most productive in history (from a financial standpoint). Yet the present generation of parents is turning around and crippling their children and grandchildren. The very lessons those from the older generations learned by not having everything they wanted, they now keep their own children from experiencing.

In many cases, we've become totally out of balance in earning money to buy all those things for our children that we didn't have. So we lose on both fronts. First, we overwork and don't spend enough time with our posterity, and second, the things we're buying them make it more difficult (if not impossible) for them to develop the character traits they need.

When I was a junior in high school I played on the high school basketball team. At that time, the athletic shoe selection wasn't great. As a matter of fact, until my junior year, the only basketball shoe available was the canvas Converse. That year, however, the leather Adidas with three black stripes came on the market. It was the "high-class" shoe.

Everybody on the team had that shoe except me. My parents couldn't afford the expensive Adidas; so I had to stick with the cheap canvas shoe. Was I deprived? I thought so then. However, I learned that the shoe had nothing to do with how I played the game. My character was enhanced by what I didn't have, and my self-worth was bolstered as I learned to deal with my peers' comments about my looking different.

I'm not implying that I couldn't have learned these same lessons by having the expensive Adidas. However, not having money may make it easier to teach our children some of the trade-offs in life that are important for them to develop social capital. When my own boys were in athletics, I could afford to buy them Nike Air shoes, and it would have been all right to do that. But then again, maybe it would be better not to buy them. The issue is this: Whether we have money or not, we need to teach our children they can't have everything they want. Therefore, even if I have a lot of wealth, I may need to make decisions as if I do not.

I hope you get the point. If you're in a vocation that doesn't generate a lot of income, don't despair. It may be easier for you to build character traits into your children than if you have a lot of extra money. If you do, be warned that you need to be very careful how you use it. Earning and spending your money with balance in mind is the key to building social capital into your children.

Foundation of Values

Now, don't overreact to these comments and move into an apartment, give away the car, and starve your children so you can teach them how to be hungry and adapt to tough times! Don't make them wear old or torn clothes so they will be ridiculed and thus have to develop the character qualities to deal with deprivation. We just need to make sure we are using our money positively and not allowing it to be a detriment to our families.

If we don't build positive character qualities into our children, we will continue to see a decline in our society. In an interesting article written several years ago for *World* magazine, Chuck Colson stated it this way: "The values erosion is largely responsible for the economic problems now facing the nation."[2] He illustrated this by noting that an epidemic of crime is costing billions, family breakdowns are costing billions more, and abandonment of the work ethic has meant loss of billions in productivity.

Good values are foundational to any society. I hope we never see a day when we have deteriorated to the point of having no focus on values at all.

∽ FOR FURTHER REFLECTION ∽

1. Have you ever said you want your children to have it better than you did? Do you still feel that way? Why or why not?

2. In what ways did you learn how to work as a child?

3. In what ways are you helping your children learn a positive work ethic? In what ways could you enhance their understanding of this concept and, subsequently, instill the character qualities of responsibility and discipline?

4. Do you agree that it is potentially more difficult to teach a good work ethic and help your children learn trade-offs if you have money than if you don't?

10

An Alternative Investment, Part 1

Investing in the Social and Spiritual Capital of Your Children

If I would get to the highest place in Athens, I would lift up my voice to say, "What mean you, fellow citizens, that you turn every stone to scrape wealth together, and take so little care of your children to whom you must one day relinquish it all?"

SOCRATES, 469 BC

We must have room to breathe. We need freedom to think and permission to heal. Our relationships are being starved to death by velocity. No one has time to listen, let alone love. Our children lay wounded on the ground, run over by our high-speed good intentions.

RICHARD SWENSON

He established a testimony in Jacob, and appointed a law in Israel, which He commanded our fathers, that they should make them known to their children; that the generation to come might know them, the children who would be born, that they may arise and declare them to their children, that they may set their hope in God, and not forget the works of God, but keep His commandments.

PSALM 78:5-7

In the last two chapters, we have looked at components of spiritual and social capital and unpacked some ways to build them into our children. In this chapter, we will look at some specific ways to invest and use financial capital to build both spiritual and social capital into our children.

I have been in the financial services industry for almost four decades. In our industry, the use of the term *investment* usually refers to conventional financial instruments like stocks, bonds, and cash. And the term *alternative investment* refers to an asset that is not conventional. It is complex in nature and has limited regulation. The most common alternative investments are private equity, real estate, hedge funds, and commodities. Alternatives tend to have attributes that differ from typical stock and bond investments from a return and time-horizon perspective.

So why am I explaining types of investments? Because in this chapter, I hope to inspire and challenge you to consider a different type of alternative investment—an investment in your children. From a return and time-horizon perspective, I don't think you will regret doing this.

Posterity Investments

Most of us have never considered any type of investment other than the ones traditionally mentioned—stocks, bonds, cash, etc. When I've had margin or surplus or savings to invest, I've put it into a financial instrument—either a personal investment account, a retirement plan, or to pay off debt (which is still a financial capital investment). It wasn't until I began to understand the concepts regarding posterity versus prosperity that I began to realize that any margin I had could potentially go into an investment in my posterity. So rather than thinking only about personal or retirement plan investing or paying off debt, I also thought about the concept of a posterity investment.

What exactly does this mean? Rather than always defaulting to the traditional financial investments, Julie and I began to ask the question,

"Is there a way to use some of this money to better build spiritual and social capital into our children?" The result was a line in our budget called "posterity," which was a predetermined amount from our surplus that was earmarked to invest in posterity. Just like you may predetermine to put $2,000 in an IRA, you can predetermine an amount to invest in your children. By considering this ahead of time and earmarking it for posterity, this amount will not end up being allocated to traditional investments.

Before getting into some of the ways one could invest in posterity, let me state a disclaimer. Some of you reading this book do *not* have a surplus to invest in *any* investment category (financial or posterity). You are just surviving from paycheck to paycheck and are hoping you can accumulate some personal savings and someday put away a little bit of your money for retirement. If that describes you, do not be discouraged. As I have mentioned many times in this book and observed over a period of four decades, in many cases, our kids are better off if we do not shower them with our surplus. For our children to have to learn to work builds character, resilience, and social capital; and they will also learn to trust God, which builds spiritual capital.

Not having surplus when raising a young family is not necessarily a negative. Being in that situation can teach you and your children many great lessons about contentment. As a matter of fact, we are told in Psalm 78:5-7 that fathers are to teach their children to put their confidence in God, to not forget the works of God, and to keep His commandments. Many times, building this kind of trust is more difficult when you have a surplus. So take heart if you do not have margin. God has your situation and your family in His hands. But if you do have a surplus (and it is my observation that most people do, given how many people have funds in a retirement account), then the rest of this chapter is for you and will help you look at alternative ways to invest.

*For our children to have to learn
to work builds character, resilience,
and social capital; and they
will also learn to trust God,
which builds spiritual capital.*

Alternative Investments

In the past, I would have considered many of these suggested investments an expense rather than an investment. Many of them might appear to increase your living expenses (such as your food budget) or they may seem to be a frivolous use of money (gas for the boat), but as you will see, the outflow included a spiritual and social purpose. As a result, these were categorized as posterity investments rather than as expenses. They were funded out of margin or surplus and did not increase our normal living expenses. They were also not necessarily made each year. We decided on these investments on a year-by-year basis.

Summer steak dinners. Julie and I have three boys, and they eat a lot! One summer we hosted a college athlete in our home. All four of the boys were into weightlifting and increasing their muscle mass. To encourage them to eat healthy and avoid some of the trendy supplements their friends were taking, Julie and I decided we would buy steak and other high-protein foods for them. The high-priced foods, plus an extra mouth to feed, increased our food budget $1,000 per month. We invested $3,000 that summer so the boys could eat healthy, minister to one of their friends, and create memories they will not soon forget.

After all, the way to a boy's heart is through his stomach. This leads to another alternative investment.

Stocked pantry. We decided we preferred for our boys and their friends to hang out at our house as much as possible. One way we encouraged that was to have an "open pantry and fridge" policy. All food and snacks at our house were free game for the boys and their friends. Many times they were like locusts, and although this increased our food costs $100-200 per month, ultimately, this was an investment in our posterity and their friends. Their presence in our home allowed us to eat meals together, share spiritual nuggets, and get to know their friends better. This is a great investment for teenage and early college-age children.

Mission trips. We discussed this briefly in chapter 8—paying for a trip to a third-world country is a great way to expose your children to what God is doing in the world, give them some perspective on their own lives, and hopefully build their spiritual capital. Julie and I travelled to Brazil and Paraguay with our boys to expose them to other parts of the world and spend quality time with them away from the distractions of home. Each trip cost us approximately $3,000, but we decided that was a good use of surplus. Sure, we could have put that money into an IRA or another financial investment, but then we considered what we were trying to build (social and spiritual capital). That led us to consider the mission trips an investment, and they were not just an expense, but a life-changing experience.

Car match. We told our boys we would match what they saved for a car if they earned a college scholarship. This investment accomplished a couple of things. First, the scholarship incentive motivated them to keep their grades up, which required them to build discipline, follow through, learn responsibility, and develop other skills needed to excel academically (social capital investment). Second, the car savings motivated them to work on weekends and in the summer so they could accumulate cash in their car fund. As we discussed earlier, there are many social capital traits learned from working hard, so this was a great alternative investment for us to put into place for our sons.

Book reports. I shared with my boys that I believe "leaders are readers." Unfortunately, in today's technology-based society, reading is a lost art. It is reported that most children read fewer than 15 minutes a day.[1] To give our children incentive to read, I gave them a list of great books and paid them $100 for each book report they completed. These books aimed to build spiritual capital—books like *Knowing God, Knowledge of the Holy, Saving Life of Christ, Decision Making and the Will of God,* and *Pursuit of God.* I also included books on scheduling, business, finances, and marriage to build their social capital—books like *Margin, Balancing Life's Demands, Men and Marriage, The Mystery of Marriage, Master Your Money, The Treasure Principle, Start with Why, The Barbarian Way, The Truth About Money Lies, What Makes a Leader Great,* and *Your Money Made Simple.* Our oldest son read 30 books in his college years, so we were happy to invest $3,000 in him. Our other sons weren't quite as prolific. We have kept this alternative investment in our financial plan and we included our daughters-in-law when the boys got married.

Trips home or to see each other. As our sons got married and started their careers, they moved away from Atlanta. When they were getting started, money was tight for them, so Julie and I knew it would be difficult for them to afford to make it back to Atlanta to visit, especially if they needed to fly. So we invested in making it a zero-cost trip for them to come home for a family reunion or holiday. In other words, if we requested that they come home, then we paid for their travel expenses, such as airplane tickets or gas money. We also wanted to encourage our boys to maintain their close relationships with each other even after they were married. So recently we invested in paying lodging costs for three nights for each of them if they all wanted to get away together as couples.

Before I share any additional alternative investments, let me say this: There is a fine line between indulging, enabling, and coddling our children as opposed to investing in them. It will take wisdom on your part (ask God, who will give you wisdom liberally—James 1:5-8) to discern the difference. If you are in doubt as you consider making an alternative investment like the ones suggested here, you could ask a trusted mentor for input or advice. Most likely you already seek financial counsel on how to invest in traditional financial investments, so why not get some advice for your alternative posterity investments as well?

Leisure activities. Julie and I were fortunate to be able to buy a used boat. You may be thinking, *And you are a financial expert? Don't you know a boat is a money pit?* Well, I would have been in that camp of thinking as well, except for the idea that this investment would allow us to invest in our sons and their friends at a formative time in their lives. With that mindset, the boat became an investment in posterity, and for almost 20 years, we have used it in a variety of ways to build social and spiritual capital. For example, Julie used it for a church summer camp; my son used it at camp when he was a counselor; and we have taken countless couples, families (primarily when their children were in their teen years), and Bible study groups to the lake with us. Gas cost about $25 per hour, but looking at this as an investment has made the cost worthwhile.

Camping equipment. When our sons were younger, we decided camping would be a good family activity for building the character traits we were trying to develop in them. I was shocked to learn how much camping equipment costs! Tent, sleeping bags, sleeping pads, cooking supplies, lanterns...it all adds up. Some of this equipment you may be able to borrow or find secondhand. Had I considered this strictly an expense, I would never have made the investment, and we would have missed out on all the memories we created over the years during our camping trips.

Yard help and equipment. As I mentioned earlier, paying for a yard service when the children are younger helps you to buy time to be with them rather than spending all Saturday mowing and doing other yard work. However, when your kids get older, maybe the investment is *not* in hiring someone to do your yard work, but instead, you buying the equipment (making the investment) and then letting your children do the work. Our boys earned funds (for the car match mentioned earlier) by setting up their own lawn businesses using the equipment we had invested in.

Summer camps. Over the years, we invested in different types of summer camp experiences. One year we went to a family Christian camp in Colorado. This trip allowed our family to be together and enabled us to build spiritual capital into our boys. Another year we went on a high-adventure camp in the north Georgia mountains. If your children are younger, you could invest in a week at a local day camp or Vacation Bible School. These can help you in your efforts to build spiritual and social capital into your kids. Here again, it can be helpful to view the cost as an investment rather than an expense.

Concert tickets. As I wrap up these suggested alternative investments, I want to share how one of my colleagues invested in his posterity. He knew his daughters wanted to attend a certain concert but could not afford to buy the tickets. He decided to surprise them by gifting them with tickets. This surplus could have gone into a financial investment or retirement account; instead, it went toward blessing and encouraging his daughters and creating a night of memories together.

Marriage weekends for grown children. As our boys have gotten older, we have invested in paying for them to attend a marriage weekend retreat so they can build up their marriages. With hotel costs, conference registration fees, and travel expenses, attending these can run $500-1,000 for the weekend. Usually this kind of money is not in the budget for a newly married couple. Our assistance has removed this barrier and will hopefully pay dividends in healthy marriages for the future.

Other ideas: You might be able to invest in your posterity by funding their educational expenses—perhaps helping your son or daughter go back for an advanced degree or paying for private school for kids or grandkids when they are in their most formative years. Look for creative ways to pour your resources into the next generation.

Big Idea

The subtitle of this book is *The Eternal Rewards of Investing Yourself and Your Money in Your Family.* The only way to accomplish this is to add a posterity investment component to your budget. I have shared a few of the alternative investments Julie and I have made to challenge your thinking and to give you some illustrations of potential investments. This list is in no way exhaustive or prescriptive. There are as many alternative posterity investments as there are unique situations and families. Tailor your ideas to the ages and interests of your family. Think of what activities you enjoy and what benefits or memories you would like to pass on to them.

Remember the definition of an alternative investment: complex, not conventional, and different with a long-time horizon. That concept is the key. You are making these investments to build a long-term return in spiritual and social capital in your posterity. These investments may be unconventional or unpopular, and your friends and family may even scoff at you for not putting the money in traditional investments with a focus on retirement and taking care of yourself financially. But let me encourage you: As I look back at our spending, I have no regrets that we made these investments in our family. We might have ended up with more financial capital had we invested differently, but seeing the social and spiritual capital returns in the lives of our sons is priceless and cannot be quantified on a balance sheet.

I hope you have captured the BIG IDEA that if you have a surplus, then before you automatically default to traditional investments, consider ways to invest in your children's spiritual and social capital. In the appendix at the end of this book is a more exhaustive list of the spiritual and social capital components that Julie and I poured into our children, and these guidelines gave us ideas for potential ways we could make alternative investments. If we saw a characteristic or benefit we were trying to develop and there was a way to invest in it financially, then we were not reticent to invest. Looking back, I am confident that our alternative investments in social and spiritual capital have resulted in greater returns than we ever could have imagined.

⟶ FOR FURTHER REFLECTION ⟵

1. Are you like Julie and Russ, with a tendency to default toward traditional financial investments? Why do you think that is?

2. What is the distinction between a posterity investment and an expense?

3. Given the ages of your children, can you think of some appropriate posterity investments you can make for the purpose of building social and spiritual capital?

4. Is this type of alternative investing difficult for you to consider? Why or why not?

11

An Alternative Investment, Part 2
Investing in Your Marriage

*God created man in His own image, in the image of God He
created him; male and female He created them.
Then God blessed them; and God said to
them, "Be fruitful and multiply."*
GENESIS 1:27-28

*A man shall leave his father and mother and be joined
to his wife, and they shall become one flesh.*
GENESIS 2:24

*The highest happiness on earth is in marriage. Every
man who is happily married is a successful man
even if he has failed in everything else.*
WILLIAM LYON PHELPS

If you're like me, you've probably had a time in your marriage where
your wife had a commitment out of town and was gone for a day or
two and you had to take care of everything. And like me, you probably

thought doing that would be no problem. You could handle the home and family with no sweat, right?

That was what I thought when Julie had to attend a funeral out of town and needed to be gone for a couple of days. I uttered the infamous words, "No problem. Don't worry. I can handle it."

Well, I did handle her 48-hour absence—but just barely. I was able to get the kids to school, feed them, and even get a little work done at the office. But that was it. I did not do any laundry, buy any groceries, schedule any appointments, or do any of the other activities Julie does to make our household run smoothly. I also didn't help much with homework or sit and read to our boys, or spend much time listening to them or answering their questions as she always did. I didn't take the time to strategically train and pour values into them as Julie did, which, as we know by now, is so important.

Needless to say, after those 48 hours, I had a renewed appreciation for all that Julie does and for the importance of teamwork in the area of posterity development. That's why marriages are so critically important as we raise the next generation.

In this chapter we will look at the role marriage plays not only in the development of a godly posterity, but also in the accumulation of financial capital. We will look at how we can use our money to enhance our marriages and maximize time with our children.

Posterity Implications

We've spent a lot of time looking at the importance of balancing work and family so we can have time to invest in our posterity. I believe that one of the best ways to invest in our children is to spend time growing and maintaining a harmonious marriage. Why? Because one of the best things we can do for our kids is keep our marriages together and model for them the relationship between Christ and the church (Ephesians 5:22-33). Harmonious marriages give our children a healthy and secure environment in which they can grow to be productive and godly members of society.

Now, for a variety of reasons, you may be facing life as a single parent. I realize that bearing the responsibility and joy of raising children on your own can be daunting and exhausting. My heart goes out to you because often you need to perform both mom and dad roles with little support. My advice is to meet with your pastor or a faith-based support group and use the church body and your extended family to help with the task of raising children. Trust that God knows your heart's desires for your children, and that He will grant you wisdom and help on this journey.

For our family, Julie and I felt it was best to embrace the model of the husband working outside the home and the wife staying at home. For some women, being a stay-at-home mom is a divine assignment. I like what Dorothy Patterson says in the book *Recovering Biblical Manhood and Womanhood*:

> The home was once described as "a place apart, a walled garden, in which certain virtues too easily crushed by modern life could be preserved," and the mother in this home was described as "The Angel in the House." Few women realize what great service they are doing for mankind and for the kingdom of Christ when they provide a shelter for the family and good mothering—the foundation on which all else is built. A mother builds something far more magnificent than any cathedral—the dwelling place for an immortal soul (both her child's fleshly tabernacle and his earthly abode). No professional pursuit so uniquely combines the most menial tasks with the most meaningful opportunities...
>
> The result of really competent mothering will be passed from generation to generation. Products in the marketplace may come and go, but generation after generation we produce our sons and daughters. A child needs his mother to be all there; to be focused on him, to recognize his problems and needs; to support, guide, see, listen to him, love and want him.[1]

Yes, motherhood is indeed a high calling and a time-consuming and demanding job. That's why I believe that moms must have the importance of their role affirmed.

Not every family will want to or be able to follow the path that Julie and I chose. In today's world, there are countless combinations of home life: single working parents, both parents working, one parent works while the other goes to school, the wife works and the husband stays home, or one parent works full-time while the other works part-time.

Ultimately, building a foundation of spiritual and social capital requires couples to work together as a team to develop and maintain harmony in a marriage, which is not always easy. For two people to desire and seek to live as one is hard. We must put aside our selfish desires and learn empathy and respect for our spouse, knowing that our children are watching and listening. They are learning what loves is, what marriage looks like, and what they should look for in a spouse one day. They are seeking peace, assurance, and secure attachment. In this chapter, we will look at some ways to invest in your marriage and, by so doing, build a solid foundation upon which your children can flourish.

Live on One Income

In our company, we frequently help couples create a financial plan to live on one income. As we saw earlier in the book, this decision is critical when it comes to deciding to purchase a home, but it is also critical in regards to marriage and investing in the spiritual and social capital of children. The key is realizing that posterity is worth the sacrifice of living on less income and then making the best financial choices to support the decision you've made. A financial plan will often show that a second income is eroded by increased expenses such as commuting, car repairs, childcare, clothing and dry-cleaning expenses, federal and state taxes, and eating out, etc.

Depending on your income tax bracket and the increased expenses noted above, a second income—at best—contributes only 50 percent of its gross income to a family's net spendable income, and in many cases, the incremental contribution is only 25 to 35 percent, if that. The point is that couples should think carefully when they calculate how much actual spendable income the second salary will generate. They may find that cutting current expenses or waiting until the kids are in school (thus saving on costly childcare expenses) are better alternatives to making ends meet.

When Julie and I got married, I was a schoolteacher, and she was a nurse anesthetist. She made twice what I made, but we committed to living on my income and saving her income (after taxes and giving). Although it was difficult to live on one income and the budget was tight, this financial discipline gave us a solid foundation to build upon. We learned that if getting by is hard early on, then it will get easier later. But if you make it easy on yourself early, then exercising such discipline will get harder later. It is very easy to get in the habit of living on both incomes at first, then feeling trapped later because it is difficult for you to decrease your lifestyle expenses, especially if you haven't saved cash or have taken on car loans and credit card debt. Living on one income and saving the other can set you up for financial freedom in the future. Financial maturity is forgoing current desires for future rewards and benefits.

I know this concept is not easy to live out. You will most likely look different than your friends who are living on two incomes, drive new cars, travel often, and have their children in daycare. I've been there. Julie and I drove old cars, did not have a dining room table for years while we saved up money, did not go on lavish vacations, and did not eat out very much. But now, fast-forward decades later, and we have financial freedom, close relationships with our children, and do not regret our lower household income or our posterity investments over the years. Many of our friends whose lifestyle choices required two incomes now regret the time they missed with their children during those early, formative years.

One of the most critical benefits of living on one income with one spouse at home is the ability to slow the pace of life and enjoy the journey. Life goes by fast enough, and if we aren't careful, then we can miss out on countless wonderful opportunities with our spouse and children. It is my observation that when both spouses work outside the home, the pace of life increases. Errands and home chores get moved to the weekend and place stress upon those two "days off" as well.

Stephen Covey, in his book *7 Habits of Highly Effective People*, says one of his seven principles is to "begin with the end mind." What is your end goal? Is it to retire early with a large retirement account? Or is it to enjoy each day to the fullest and truly delight in the people around you—especially your family?

Ways to Invest in Your Marriage

It is wise for us to use our money to invest in our marriage and promote the spiritual and emotional well-being of our spouse. This use of money should be considered an alternative investment with one of the highest returns we will ever get. Some people are diligent about investing their money in real estate, the stock market, and their businesses, yet they fail to use some of their funds to enhance their marriage.

There are several ways you can make this alternative investment. One way, as we have seen, is to be willing to forego some income and buy more time to spend together. Work four days a week instead of five, or opt for more vacation time instead of an annual raise. Replace work time with quality time with your spouse. Remember the principle of time replacement? When I get overloaded at work and have several late nights in succession, or when I'm late for dinner (or miss it entirely), I feel like I have missed out. When that happens, Julie and I don't have a chance to catch up on our day, talk about life, or think through our schedules. Not being able to intentionally talk together about the issues of life and family reduces our oneness. By being more conscious of my time and guarding the delicate work/life balance, I'm investing in my relationship with my wife.

Make time to pray together, study the Bible together, and enjoy the fellowship of other couples. We also need to make sure our work doesn't intrude on our daily quiet time with God. If you were to ask your spouse right now whether he or she would rather you invest more in the stock market or invest some of your time in a Bible study, I think I know what the response will be.

Another way to invest in your spouse is to spend money when the circumstances dictate that buying more time to invest in your marriage makes sense. Many times during the year (especially around the holiday season), Julie and I hire a cleaning service to help out with tasks around the home. This positively affects our family and frees up some time for us to invest in one another. Sometimes I would come home early from work and watch the kids so Julie could go to a movie with a friend or out to dinner. All of these options require an expenditure of money, yet we shouldn't view such costs as expenses, but alternative investments. The return on your relationship will be worth it.

We can also invest in our spouses by planning a surprise night out or purchasing a special gift for them when they least expect it. The issue isn't what you do; it's that you realize the need to invest in and spend quality time alone with your spouse. This investment is time, first and foremost, but will also include money. Be careful not to overwork, burning the candle at both ends, to earn more money to invest in financial vehicles without also using some of those earnings to invest in relationships as well. Overworking may cause you to miss out on amazing moments in day-to-day life, and it could risk you losing the one you have committed your life to and would like to retire with. Why not go home from work a little early tomorrow night, play with the kids, help with the dinner dishes, and relax together and talk? That would make for a more memorable night for all of you.

You may be surprised to know that the amount of your financial net worth doesn't mean a thing next to what really matters. Why? Because your greatest asset—your spouse's love and support—isn't listed on a financial balance sheet. You need to spend as much time thinking through your spouse investment strategy as you do your retirement investment strategy. You will receive a greater return in eternity by spending money on your spouse than by buying another stock.

A Planning Weekend

One of the greatest investments I have ever made in my marriage is to invest in a planning weekend. By that I mean a weekend that is set aside for Julie and I to get away (without children) for the purpose of communicating and taking inventory of our relationship. By setting up such a weekend for you and your spouse, you can take the time to thoughtfully discuss issues such as your finances, children, work, goals, and dreams.

Below is a suggested format for a planning weekend. Although your schedule may vary, this example encourages you to make sure you maintain a balance between work and play.

Sample Planning Weekend Agenda

Topics: Finances, children, church (spiritual), social, work, major decisions (school for kids, changing jobs, moving to a different house), dreams, etc.

Friday	2:00-4:00	Arrive
	4:00-6:00	Rest and unwind
	6:00-	Dinner and discuss a topic listed above
Saturday	8:00-10:00	Breakfast and time alone with God
	10:00-12:00	Discuss a new topic or continue previous discussion
	12:00-5:00	Lunch, shop, recreation, etc.
	6:00-	Dinner and discuss a topic
Sunday	8:00-10:00	Breakfast and time alone with God
	10:00-12:00	Discuss action steps to promote and enhance marriage

A caution is in order here: When you go on a planning weekend, expect to do some work and come away with one or two specific action steps that will enhance your relationship. Usually both of you have been busy with the children or work and, when you get away, you'll see the trip as a great opportunity to relax, watch football, and shop—anything except plan. You don't want to inadvertently neglect the desired goal of discussing issues that you set out to resolve.

Therefore, it's important to set an agenda beforehand and commit yourselves to accomplishing the desired goals. If you happen to start discussing a very strategic issue that must be addressed at length, you may decide to stay on that issue for the entire weekend. What's important is that you accomplish at least one or two specific things that will work toward making your relationship better.

To illustrate what can happen if expectations are not adjusted before the planning weekend, let me share about what happened to Julie and me at the beginning of one such weekend. We had set aside time for this several weeks in advance, and I had anxiously looked forward to our time together to discuss some key issues related to handling our finances and raising our kids. Being the planning type, I saw no reason to wait until we arrived at our destination to begin discussing some of the issues that I knew we were going to talk about. We hadn't driven more than twenty-five minutes (it was a two-hour drive) when I began to ask Julie some planning questions to get her input.

Needless to say, she didn't respond with much enthusiasm, and after a short period of time, she said, "I can't believe it! We just left home, and you are already planning. I need time to unwind first."

At that moment, we both realized that a planning weekend can only be a success if both husband and wife have the same expectations about it. It is neither a weekend of fun and games nor a weekend of intense, unrelenting work. Rather, it is an artfully crafted time that allows you to do some work as well as enjoy being with one another.

The marital intimacy checklist at the end of this chapter is a practical tool you can use as a springboard to start the communication process at the beginning of your planning weekend. Julie and I typically answer each of the questions individually and then get together and share our answers with each other. If there are any areas in which we have significant differences in how we perceive unity, then that is where we start talking. For example, on financial intimacy, if she has a 1 and I have a 5, then obviously we are perceiving the situation from dramatically different viewpoints, and we realize that's something we need to discuss. But if we have basically the same numbers in a given area, then we do not focus on it as much as other areas.

A planning weekend will typically require a financial investment. Although you could keep costs down by getting someone to watch your kids while you have your weekend at home, that scenario is not ideal. It is usually best to get away for a couple of nights at a hotel, bed and breakfast, or friend's cabin. You need a place that will allow you some uninterrupted time for true relaxation and a break from the usual distractions. In addition to lodging, you will have travel and food expenses. The weekend may cost several hundred dollars, but Julie and I have found that the cost is well worth the benefits of the weekend.

Investing in Good Communication

A second way to invest in your marriage is to develop a plan to communicate. Unlike the planning weekend, this investment requires developing a process at no financial expense. I can definitely say, however, that this is one of the greatest investments you can make in your marriage. Prior to getting married, Julie's dad gave us this ominous warning, "If you don't have a game plan for handling conflict, you will never make it." Wow! What a way to start a marriage. But that comment set us on a path to develop a process for handling conflict. The system I describe in the upcoming paragraphs has served us well for 40 years and it has served as a great investment. I hope you will gain some insights from our process that will encourage you to come up with your own biblical game plan for handling conflict.

As you read through this section, refer to the communication flowchart on page 168. The first step is to take the time to become a student of your spouse—to understand how he or she responds to frustrating circumstances and conflict. Each of us has a certain set of "indicators" we exhibit when we are frustrated or upset about something. Understanding temperament and differences can help us to be more perceptive of those indicators. If you don't know your spouse's indicators, ask him or her.

When Julie is upset, one of her indicators is that she becomes very quiet and loses her sense of humor. Whenever I am upset, I usually respond by changing the subject or talking about side issues. When either of us exhibits these indicators, Julie and I know that we need to communicate about something.

Once those indicators have surfaced, it's important for us to be sensitive to them. Too often they are ignored, which can lead to conflict later. There are two ways you can show sensitivity. First, you can respond to the indicator you see in your spouse's behavior with a question such as, "Is something bothering you?" Asking this shows that you have noticed the indicator and are being sensitive to it. Second, if you are the one who is upset and your spouse is not picking up on the indicator, then it's your responsibility to tell him or her. If Julie is not picking up on my frustration, then I should go ahead and tell her that something is bothering me.

As you can see from the flowchart, one of our basic ground rules is that any problem must be discussed before the sun goes down (Ephesians 4:26). This practice avoids potentially greater problems that can occur when small frustrations are not dealt with in a timely manner. The issue must be discussed before bedtime.

Once the indicator has been acknowledged and there is agreement that a problem needs to be resolved, you can begin to talk about it. In most cases, it is easy for one spouse to ask, "Is something wrong?" and the other to say no when the answer is really yes. "No" is the typical first response. It takes a sensitive, consistent, and perceptive spouse to continue to gently probe until the frustration is revealed. If you know (or take the time to find out) your spouse's indicators, you'll know whether there is a problem or not. You will not be easily sidetracked by the quick no that is initially uttered.

Consider this illustration: The husband arrives home from work and, unbeknownst to him, his wife had an unpleasant run-in with another mom at soccer practice. She's annoyed and not in a good mood. He picks up on this as he thumbs through the mail, so he asks her if anything is wrong. She says, "No, it's nothing." Husbands often accept the no and go on about their own business, then wonder why their spouse is so distant and curt the rest of the evening. It is much better to gently take the time to draw the situation out and allow the other person to express his or her frustrations.

You will also note on the flowchart that in some cases it is appropriate to wait to discuss the problem. If we are having dinner at my in-law's and I notice that my wife is upset about something, that is probably not the appropriate time to deal with the problem. It's better to wait until we are alone at home, but before we go to bed that night.

There are three additional ground rules, and they are not always easy to follow.

First, don't raise your voice. Tensions can rise quickly in difficult situations, and raising our voices usually makes things worse. It's better to take a step back (mentally and physically) and use a tone that we would like to be on the receiving end of. Or, as the Bible instructs, we must be quick to listen, slow to speak, and slow to anger (James 1:19).

Second, don't provoke or antagonize. One spouse bringing up issues from the past or intentionally baiting the other doesn't benefit the situation or the marriage. Marriage is based on mutual love and respect. We should seek to treat others the way we want to be treated. This is particularly true with our spouse!

Third, don't make derogatory remarks. Sometimes when Julie shares why she is frustrated, my first thought is to say something like, "I can't believe you said that." That kind of remark will only put the other person on the defensive and break down the communication lines even more.

If any of these ground rules are broken, then the discussion is sure to go nowhere, and you should separate for a set amount of time (we recommend no longer than one hour). The purpose of this time apart is for each of you to take time to pray alone to God, praying as David did in Psalm 139:23-24: "Search me, O God, and know my heart; try me, and know my anxieties; and see if there is any wicked way in me, and lead me in the everlasting way." Then come back together to discuss the situation again. During your time apart, you will often find that the dispute is just as much your problem as it is your spouse's problem.

Take the time to be thoughtful, persistent, talk, and pray together. It's worth the effort. My wife and I have been up very late a number of times working through a problem, but it is always such a joy to have a problem resolved before we go to bed. Over the years, we have found that when conflicts are worked through, they become stepping-stones to a stronger marriage. If problems are allowed to fester and grow day after day, the oneness and unity of the relationship will become more and more disrupted.

Anytime you discuss a problem, always make sure you determine some specific action steps you can take to resolve it. In the area of finances, for example, many frustrations occur when there is no cash-flow control system. In such a situation, a specific action step to restore harmony might be to set up a budget and—with the input of both spouses—assign specific areas of responsibility. If investments are the frustration point, then perhaps a commitment is needed to discuss options before any final decision is made.

The bottom-line goal in communicating is to establish a closer and more harmonious relationship. To that end, there are two scenarios you want to avoid.

First, don't settle for a stalemate. It is not healthy for a couple to leave an issue unresolved or for the husband and wife to remain on opposite sides of an issue. I know some would say that they have agreed to disagree, but I would question how much harmony can result from that—after all, decisions still have to be made. If you are at an impasse, then perhaps it is time to use a tool such as a decision-making matrix that takes the emotion out of the decision or seek wise counsel from a trusted mentor. At Ronald Blue Trust, we share the concept of "settlement." Once everyone has had their say, then everyone must settle with the agreed-upon decision. This is a good principle to follow in your marriage. Once you have both heard each other out and a decision is made, then move forward with it.

Second, never take revenge. First Peter 3:9 tells us to not repay evil for evil, but rather, to give a blessing instead. Therefore, if one spouse makes a decision that the other spouse is not comfortable with (a bad investment or poor planning, for instance), he or she should not frivolously spend money or make an equally bad decision just to get even. Harmony is much more important than being right or winning an argument. In a marriage, we are not competitors, but teammates.

Communication Flowchart

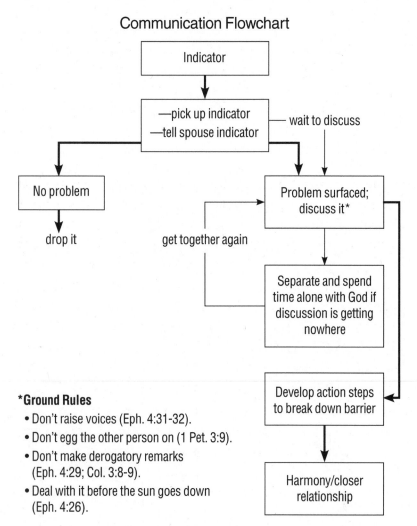

*Ground Rules
- Don't raise voices (Eph. 4:31-32).
- Don't egg the other person on (1 Pet. 3:9).
- Don't make derogatory remarks (Eph. 4:29; Col. 3:8-9).
- Deal with it before the sun goes down (Eph. 4:26).

The Financial Implications of Divided Families

When a marriage fails, there are dramatic implications to that couple's posterity and their subsequent spiritual and social capital, and there can also be implications for their financial capital. For example, the general rule is that for families with children, breaking into two separate homes increases household costs by about 30%.

The greatest security children can have is knowing that mom and dad are living in harmony.

Unfortunately, divided families are a reality in our culture. When that happens, the financial capital of the former marriage partners is dissipated due to the increased cash flow needed to support more than one household. Also, when the financial capital is ultimately distributed through the estate, it's almost always difficult to sort everything out, and in most cases messy due to the different family units and competing interests involved. However, the erosion of financial capital is less of a concern than the negative impact on the former couple's posterity.

Our posterity can suffer when our marriages fall apart. The greatest security children can have is knowing that mom and dad are living in harmony. No amount of money can replace a good marriage.

For Further Reflection

1. If you and your spouse are both employed outside the home, what would you need to do financially to live on one income?

2. In what ways can you invest financially in your spouse?

3. Do your children witness a harmonious marriage they want to emulate? In what ways can you increase your harmony?

4. What one thing could you do now to improve your marriage?

Marital Intimacy Checklist

As you review your marriage, how would you evaluate *your* degree of satisfaction with the following items? Circle the number that best describes your feelings.

		Very Dissatisfied	Somewhat Dissatisfied	Neutral	Somewhat Satisfied	Very Satisfied
1.	**Spiritual Intimacy** *(oneness before God)*	1	2	3	4	5
2.	**Work Intimacy** *(sharing common tasks)*	1	2	3	4	5
3.	**Intellectual Intimacy** *(closeness in ideas)*	1	2	3	4	5
4.	**Recreational Intimacy** *(relating in fun and play)*	1	2	3	4	5
5.	**Emotional Intimacy** *(being on same wavelength)*	1	2	3	4	5
6.	**Crisis Intimacy** *(closeness in problems and pain)*	1	2	3	4	5
7.	**Conflict Intimacy** *(understanding in facing and struggling with differences)*	1	2	3	4	5
8.	**Creative Intimacy** *(sharing in acts of creating together)*	1	2	3	4	5
9.	**Commitment Intimacy** *(common benefits from shared efforts)*	1	2	3	4	5
10.	**Aesthetic Intimacy** *(sharing experiences of beauty)*	1	2	3	4	5
11.	**Sexual Intimacy**	1	2	3	4	5
12.	**Communication Intimacy** *(feeling of openness in every area)*	1	2	3	4	5
13.	**Financial Intimacy** *(communication on finances)*	1	2	3	4	5

After each spouse responds separately, get together and discuss why you responded the way you did.

Reproduced by permission of Ron Blue Trust, Atlanta, GA

Contentment: Productive vs. Consumptive

Leaving Financial Capital for Your Children

The almighty dollar bequeathed to a child is an almighty curse.
No man has the right to handicap his son with such a burden as
great wealth. He must face this question squarely: Will my fortune
be safe with my boy and will my boy be safe with my fortune?

ANDREW CARNEGIE

It is every man's duty to strive to give his children the
best possible equipment for life. But to leave millions to
young sons is dangerous. Each of us is better for having
to make our own money in the world... To take from
anyone the incentive to work is a questionable service.

A.P. GIANNINI, HEAD OF BANK OF AMERICA

Do you see a man who excels in his work? He will stand
before kings; he will not stand before unknown men.

PROVERBS 22:29

As alluded to in chapter 10, there is a fine line between using our financial capital to invest in our children versus indulging, enabling, or coddling them. Most of the posterity investments Julie and I made were possible only because our boys were taught the value of contentment and the need to be productive early in life. Teaching these lessons helped to ensure that our posterity investments were helpful and not harmful. There are many ways to teach children these lessons. In our case, here are the expectations we had for our boys:

1. They get jobs and work during high school (in the summers and after school if they did not participate in sports at school) to take advantage of the "car match" mentioned earlier. They created a lawn service business and worked at fast food restaurants, which allowed them to learn a good work ethic, industriousness, responsibility, and several other social capital character traits.

2. They earn good grades in high school so they could qualify for college scholarships.

3. They attend and graduate from college.

4. They secure jobs after college and provide for their own living expenses and needs. We taught them to live within their means and not accumulate consumer and credit card debt.

Upon accomplishing these things, our sons had proven their ability to make it on their own and not live a consumptive lifestyle. They had launched!

This last point is the biggest hurdle, and one that, unfortunately, is not being cleared by many young adults today. We are grateful that our boys achieved self-sufficiency. If you are in a different situation and there is a failure to launch, I would encourage you to make sure you are not using your financial capital to continue to enable your grown children. The situation may also require a third party to assist you in the launch sequence. (Note: there are some situations and periods of time that a delay in launch could be warranted—such as illness, short-term job market situations, a need for more education, etc.) But the goal we should set for our children is for them to become productive, contributing members of society. Don't allow your financial capital to undermine this goal.

Let's unpack some of the challenges that come with being consumptive and not being content.

Consumptive vs. Productive

The scenario is common. Working parents have been toiling away at building their financial house. They are producing wealth while also buying their children items to consume. The natural response to not feeling like we have enough time to spend with our children is to indulge them with material things. We missed their soccer game, so we stop by the store and pick up a toy for them. We couldn't be the mystery reader at school because we had an important deadline at work, so we buy them a new video game. Often without even being aware of it, children develop a consumptive worldview rather than a productive mentality. Kids may come to expect toys, electronic devices, and other trappings that wealth can buy as a requirement rather than privilege. They do not recognize the work and time that went into earning the money that pays for those items. They don't connect the parents' production to their consumption. Unfortunately, the future patterns that are set from these kinds of decisions are predictable.

Children who have learned to be consumptive rather than productive often face an interesting dilemma as young adults. When they attempt to follow their dreams and vocational interests—such as getting a job that maximizes their skills and strengths in the marketplace—they realize they cannot generate enough income to support the lifestyle to which they have become accustomed. At this crossroad, there are two options. Either take the lower-paying job that allows them to follow their dreams and work within their vocational interests and live at a lower lifestyle level, or find a job that will support the lifestyle they have come to expect. Often, they choose to seek the highest-paying jobs regardless of whether they're equipped for them or they desire to pursue those specific career paths. Thus begins a frustrating cycle of moving from one job to another trying to support consumptive desires and staying in unenjoyable jobs solely for the salary they provide.

This consumption mentality and dependence are common when a family-owned business is involved because the business usually affords the family significant income and perks. The children may have worked in the business while growing up and are expected to join it after graduation. While they may make an effort at another line of work because of their interests, if they find that vocation can't support the lifestyle they are used to, then they may default back to the family business—not because it's their passion, but because it's the best financial option. Although a consumptive mentality is often the reason for adult children migrating back to the family business, it's not the only reason. In some cases, their fear of disappointing the parents is so great that they will go back to the business even though it's not what they really want to do.

So why do parents let children come into the family business and draw a good salary even though they aren't productive or fulfilled? It may be that the parents like having them there and feel that they can lead the business into the future, thus preserving the family's financial legacy. Unfortunately, this isn't usually the end result.

Children who are in the family business just because of the money can be caught in a dangerous trap. Most likely, other employees are perceptive enough to recognize that the owner's children aren't productive enough to warrant the income they're receiving, and the heirs know it too. With no feelings of accomplishment or significance, they look for a cause that needs them or they adopt expensive hobbies or dangerous activities—like safaris, racing cars, or running marathons. They spend life trying to "find" themselves. Family business expert Leon Danco confirms this. He found that the business owners' children are usually oversold and underdeveloped. Because so many don't get the chance to do anything productive in the business, they become embittered, noneconomic beings.[1]

Children trained to be consumptive are put into the position of working in the family business so they can meet their income needs. If the family business is sold, they may find themselves unprepared for the "outside" job they'll need to find. In many cases, if they received a lump sum from the sale of the family business, the principal ends up being rapidly dissipated. Only when they run out of money do they try to be productive, but they can't because they don't know how. This situation typically leads to a life of drifting from one job to the next and barely making it from paycheck to paycheck.

Children who are dependent on the family business or handouts to support a habit of consumption are similar to those who are addicted to drugs. They're just as dependent and just as trapped. With a habit they can't break, their personal life and marriage can be affected negatively. Sadly, a contributing factor to some divorces is the inability of grown children to sever financial ties with their parents.

Many families in America have generated significant wealth only to see it lost because they raised their children to consume rather than produce. If children are taught to be productive and not consumptive, then whatever they earn vocationally will likely be adequate to support their lifestyles. They will be free to pursue a career that fits their skills, abilities, and interests. And if they do end up going into the family business, they will be better prepared to become a contributing member of the organization.

If children are taught to be productive and not consumptive, then whatever they earn vocationally will likely be adequate to support their lifestyles.

A trust fund with significant assets can have the same effect as a family business. I know a young man who spent the first 20 years of his adult life scuba diving in the summer and skiing in the winter. He has yet to live a productive day in his adult life because he expects the trust fund to provide for him. Unfortunately, the assets are significant enough that they probably will last his entire lifetime, but his children may be in for a rude awakening. They will have to be productive because there may not be any money left to pass on to them and they may not know what it means to be a hard worker whose lifestyle is determined by their skills and their salary.

This concept of consumption versus production and its corresponding problems is highlighted in Patrick Reynolds's book *The Gilded Leaf*. Patrick, the grandson of R.J. Reynolds of the Reynolds tobacco family, described his grandfather as a canny politician, a workaholic, and a farsighted risk-taker who built the family business. According to Patrick, two of R.J.'s sons, Dick and Smith, became irresponsible playboys. After four failed marriages, Dick died "a troubled recluse," leaving a confusing will that threw his family into chaos. About himself, Patrick wrote:

> I was raised with the Reynolds name—but not the family.
>
> I knew that at 21 I would inherit $2.5 million—a legacy from my grandmother. That was a mixed blessing.
>
> I developed an interest in filmmaking. But rather than work my way up in a production company, learning to be part of a group, I attended film festivals and classes, and spent hours in my expensive film editing laboratory— always alone. At first, my inherited wealth isolated me since I didn't need to get a job, depend on others, etc. Later, when I wanted work as an actor, the fact that I didn't need to work was held against me.
>
> I enjoyed a youthful period of Hollywood high-life.

Then, seeking stability, I married...and subsequently, as had become the fashion, I divorced, too.

I thought I could outdo my father and grandfather and achieve a massive fortune. But, untutored in the world of business, I made a series of bad investments. That erosion of capital finally forced me to join society.[2]

Patrick Reynolds's advice is consistent with my theory of posterity: "Provide your children with plenty of personal guidance. Spend time with them. Boarding schools cannot take the place of effective parenting. Require that they live on money they earn well into their 20s—or even their 30s. Reason: This allows them to establish a firm identity and sense of self-worth."[3]

The Blessing of Contentment

A consumptive mentality can also put pressure on couples to earn more, take on debt, or remain dependent on extended family to meet their financial needs. Further, expecting a standard of living defined by certain material things, such as the right neighborhood, clothes, and cars can breed discontentment when that lifestyle isn't achieved. This, in turn, can have several negative consequences. Spouses may overwork in an attempt to make more money to reach their desired standard of living. However, as they spend more and more time at work, they have less and less time for each other and their children, which has a negative impact on their marriage and the raising of a godly posterity. Or, as debt mounts, the pressure to work more grows and the cycle continues, or a nonworking spouse may have to find a job.

I've always appreciated Julie's attitude of contentment. She reminds me that she is happy with our lifestyle and it doesn't matter what I earn. She has told me she would be happy in a tent in Alaska (and she hates to be cold!), and that we are wealthy simply because we have each other. She doesn't put pressure on me to earn more money or buy more things. Her life exemplifies the principle of Proverbs 31:12: "She does him good and not evil all the days of her life."

I'm convinced Julie's mindset is, to a large degree, because of her dad's encouragement vocationally and because both her parents modeled a lifestyle of living within their means and being generous. Although her dad was a doctor and they could afford anything they wanted (and they did have an airplane and a boat), Julie's parents made it clear to Julie and her brother that these things were for the whole family to enjoy. She should not expect to continue to have them when she left home. They shopped at modest stores, and the children didn't always have the trendiest clothes, toys, or cars. Most important of all, Julie's parents modeled generous giving to others, which goes a long way toward slaying the consumptive mindset. They taught Julie to be thankful for what she had and to share with others who were not as fortunate.

It is not easy to instill contentment in children (or in adults) in today's world. We are bombarded with advertising and messaging about how much we deserve and how to get it quickly. The world says, "No need to wait or save or work for what we want. Just buy it now and pay later." This makes it all the more difficult for parents to teach their children the trait of contentment. The immature child wants what he wants and he wants it now—the right name-brand clothes, the newest smartphone, or the hottest car. Parents need to start at an early age to model contentment so their children can learn it as well.

In Summary: The Four Critical Needs of Adult Children

Our adult children have four critical needs so they can develop sound social and spiritual capital:

First, they must feel the freedom to have careers that are what God equips and calls them to do. They may have different goals, dreams, and aspirations than us, and they should be allowed to pursue those dreams and desires.

Second, if grown children do enter the family business, parents need to realize the boundaries between their work and personal relationships. It can be difficult to treat your son or daughter differently at work than you do at home. You should not expect more or less of them than you do of any other employee at their level. Wise parents will be careful not to put their children in awkward and compromising positions.

Third, if children want to follow in their parents' footsteps vocationally, they need to be allowed to make their own mark on the business. With their training and education, they will likely have different ideas about how processes should be handled and decisions should be made. They should be allowed to implement their ideas (or at least some of them) so they can establish an identity for themselves and a feeling of significance. Just because something has been done a certain way for 30 years doesn't mean it's the right way to do it today. In this age of increasing knowledge, evolving technology, and expanding information networks, experience isn't what it used to be. New ideas and innovations come quickly and can have a tremendous impact. Again, the key is to treat every employee the same. Your son or daughter's ideas should be heard but not weighted higher than input from others in the business.

Finally, we need to allow our grown children the room to struggle and find their own way. If a butterfly is helped out of its cocoon and not allowed to struggle its way out, it will die. The struggle is what strengthens the butterfly so it can fly. Similarly, we should be careful not to use our money to overtly enable our children or make life too easy for them so they are unable to develop their independence. Like the butterfly, they must be allowed to struggle and fly on their own. While it can be difficult to watch them do this, we must let them go.

⁓ For Further Reflection ⁓

1. What are some ways you are teaching your children to be producers instead of consumers?

2. How can you model contentment for your children?

3. Have you found that your children are different from you? If so, how?

4. If you have a family-owned business, has this chapter helped to challenge your thinking about whether your children should have a part in that business? If so, in what way?

Your Children's Children

The Financial Legacy We Leave to Coming Generations

The glory of young men is their strength, and the splendor of old men is their gray head.
PROVERBS 20:29

The silver-haired head is a crown of glory.
PROVERBS 16:31

On a beautiful spring day Grandpa and Grandma pulled into a BMW dealership.

"What color do you think Sara would like the best?" asked Grandpa.

"I don't know," answered Grandma, somewhat reserved. "I know her favorite color is yellow, but I don't know if that would be the best color for a car."

"Yes, I know what you mean," said Grandpa as he rubbed his chin with his hand, pondering what to do. "I think light blue would be a good color for her."

"Yes, light blue would be pretty. But you know, I wonder if we really ought to be doing this for her sixteenth birthday. Don't you think it is a little much?"

"No!" retorted Grandpa. "I think it is just fine. After all, she is a good kid, and you only turn sixteen once."

"You know how frugal her parents are. Don't you think we should at least run it by them first?"

"No, I don't. It is our money, and this is what I want to do. Let's go on into the sales office and get the paperwork started. I don't want this to take all day."

How much should grandparents give their grandchildren? In this chapter, I will try to help current and future grandparents decide how to make sound financial decisions regarding their grandchildren. My thoughts come from observing successful grandparents—as well as unsuccessful ones.

The "How Much?" Issue

I'm amazed at how many grandparents are unwilling to leave large sums of money to their own children because they weren't trained to manage it well, but will leave significant wealth to grandchildren who can't even talk or walk yet. These grandchildren haven't been trained in spiritual and social capital, let alone financial stewardship. Will the grandchildren manage the income well?

Gifts to grandchildren occur for several reasons. First, tax law encourages what is referred to as "generation skipping." The law allows each grandparent to leave millions of dollars in trust to the grandchildren, with the advantage of the trust funds, under certain conditions, still being available to the grandparents' children during their lifetimes. Although available to their adult children, the money is not taxed in their children's estates at their subsequent deaths. Therefore, their grandchildren could receive millions plus growth with no estate tax erosion.

Second, many grandparents use their money to buy love and acceptance from their grandchildren. They establish trusts, or custodial accounts, or make large outright gifts to remind the children and grand-children that they have provided the money for education, a down payment on a home, nice clothes, etc. They may slip the grandchild a hundred-dollar bill every time they see him or her. The trust funds, cus-todial accounts, and cash can make the grandparents feel needed and sig-nificant in their grandchildren's lives. But frequently this can also create a strain between the grandparents and parents.

Any cash gift should only be made to a grandchild after consultation with the parents.

For the most part, I recommend that grandparents not give large cash gifts or assets to their grandchildren either outright or in trust. Instead, this money should go to their adult children (the grandchil-dren's parents). Even though this recommendation may be inconsis-tent with sophisticated estate tax planning techniques, such as income shifting and generation skipping, a trust can do more harm than good to grandchildren. Since their parents don't have control over the trust's ultimate distribution, the grandchildren could develop a slothful atti-tude throughout their lives as they wait for the trust funds to be dis-tributed. (If our clients set up generation-skipping trusts, we often encourage them to name a charity as a potential beneficiary in case the parents feel the trust would be a hindrance to children who have not proven to be wise stewards.)

Outright gifts or gifts in custodial accounts can also be harmful. These funds are immediately available to the child or, in the case of custodial accounts, will be available at the age of majority (eighteen or twenty-one, depending on the state). In most cases, a young child is better off having too little money than too much. Also, if the parents are teaching the child how to be a good money manager, the grandparents' gift of a significant sum can undermine the parents' efforts. Suppose the grandchild has lost his baseball glove due to irresponsibility and now has to sacrifice to buy a new one—and then his grandpa hands him $200 unannounced.

I feel *any* cash gift should be made to a grandchild only after discussing with the parents the impact this money can have on the grandchild and agreeing on the expected use of this money (a discussion which could involve the grandchild). This doesn't mean grandparents can't give their grandchildren small cash gifts as they would toys and clothes on birthdays and Christmas. However, grandparents and parents should determine what constitutes a "small gift." For some, the allowable limit may be $20; for others it may be $100. Also, the amount may increase with the age of the grandchild. The timing of the gifts is also important. To give a grandchild $100 on his or her birthday should not pose a big problem, but to give a grandchild $100 every time the grandparents see the grandchild could be too much.

Also, normal gifts of toys and clothes for Christmas and birthdays should not be excessive and unreasonable. Excessive and unreasonable gifts teach grandchildren to be *consumptive,* creating a lifestyle expectation that may be hard for them to support when they're on their own.

Is there ever a time to leave significant cash or assets to grandchildren? Yes. Cash and/or assets can be left to grandchildren in trust, outright, or in a custodial account for a predetermined purpose—if agreed upon by the parents and grandparents. For example, the grandparents could fund the grandchild's private school and college education, as long as the grandchild's parents agree. College education and private school are two areas typically outside the traditional guidelines of parental obligation of support (food, shelter, clothing, public schooling, and medical care). I've found that help in these areas is appreciated, may build financial and social capital, and typically doesn't impact the parents' feelings of provision.

Let me offer a few guidelines about large gifts. First, the grandparents shouldn't constantly remind the parents, grandkids, or others of what they've given. Once they give the gifts, they should forget they ever did it. In some cases, grandparents have used the gifts as leverage to get the parents or grandkids to behave certain ways or do something they want the parents or grandkids to do. Real gifts don't have strings attached or create implied obligations.

Second, the grandparents' motivation to do something for the grandchildren should never be used as some form of punishment to their own children (the grandchildren's parents), which is why giving the money to the parents is better. Don't skip a generation just because you're upset with your children.

The most important considerations for grandparents when giving a gift are the potential impact on the grandchildren and the impact on their relationship with their own children (the parents).

Third, if you want to fund your grandchild's college education, the amount should be such that, with standard assumptions on earnings and education costs, the majority of the funds will be used up by the time the child finishes college. You don't want him or her to receive a significant amount of money after college or at a later date that might instill complacency or encourage a poor work ethic as they wait for their windfall of funds.

Finally, trusts or custodial accounts for grandchildren should usually be funded only if the parent (your child) has no personal need for the funds. It can be very frustrating to a parent to watch significant sums of money accumulate in a child's "education account" while the parent's goals and desires go unmet because of a lack of finances.

One couple I knew would have liked to build a different house to better meet the needs of their family. To do that on one income would have been difficult. They could have benefited from some extra money, but their parents were making gifts to the three grandchildren for education (bypassing the parents). There was more than $100,000 in a trust for the grandchildren's education, and although the parents appreciated this, they were also frustrated that those funds (or some of the funds) were unavailable as a down payment on another house.

In some situations, the grandparents don't trust the parents and feel that they must take care of the grandchildren. This thinking usually creates more problems between the parents and grandparents. This issue brings us full circle. If grandparents overworked and didn't spend time with their children while they were growing up, then those grandparents probably won't be able to leave their wealth in a way that's beneficial to all of their posterity. Therefore, though some tax benefits can be derived from giving gifts to grandchildren, these benefits are secondary. The most important considerations for grandparents when giving a gift are the potential impact on the grandchildren and the impact on their relationship with their own children (the parents).

Creative Ways to Use Your Money

Rather than showering grandchildren with money, let me offer some suggestions that are consistent with the concept of "buying time" (chapter 5) to develop a godly posterity.

Take the parents and grandchildren on a vacation. Most young couples don't have discretionary funds to take a nice vacation. If the grandparents offer to pay for the trip and include everybody, then they are investing in family memories for multiple generations. Not only will a trip together create memories, but the grandparents can spend time with the grandchildren and reinforce the values and qualities the parents are teaching them. The vacation could be traveling to the beach, going to a ski area in Colorado, or attending a family camp. It could also be as simple as paying for the parents and grandchildren to come for a visit if they live in another state.

Offer to fund private elementary and secondary school. The first ten years of a child's life are the most critical. This is also when money may be tightest for the parents. Grandparents may make a strategic investment for the grandchild to attend a private Christian school that could help develop godly spiritual and social capital in the grandchild.

Offer to find housecleaning help. When parents have young children, something as apparently insignificant as funding a housecleaning service on a regular basis could have an incredible impact on the emotional and physical strength of the household. Parents then have more energy to channel into the grandchildren at this formative time in their lives.

Invest in the grandchildren and their parents by giving of your time. Although it costs your wallet the least, perhaps the most important gift grandparents can make is to invest time in their children and grandchildren. There are numerous ways to do this. Offer to do some projects around the house that free mom and dad for more kid time. Babysit the grandchildren for an afternoon or for a weekend so the parents can get away for a date, planning session, marriage seminar, or retreat. All of these are investments in posterity.

In a society where the extended family often lives far away, the investment of time may require grandparents to use some financial resources to rent housing close to their children and grandchildren so they can spend time with them. It may require some funds for airplane tickets to visit more frequently. Or you may drive many hours to spend short amounts of time with them.

Make cash gifts if the extended family is fragmented. As we discussed in chapter 5, it is more costly today to buy time than it was when everyone's extended family was closer geographically. If you can't be there physically to give your time, some unexpected cash could be very welcome to help your children buy time to be with or invest in your grandchildren. Remember, it does cost more today to spend time together than when you were raising your children and Grandma and Grandpa were right around the corner.

Undoubtedly, grandparents can think of countless other ways to invest their time and money to enhance the posterity of the two generations that come after them. But remember, posterity is what's important, not trust funds that may leave a legacy of children and grandchildren dependent on the previous generation's wealth. Trust funds that were intended as a blessing can often have the opposite effect.

If you have already set up trusts, I encourage you to immediately begin developing values and character in your grandchildren. At the same time, don't complicate matters by leaving even more to them. If you have chosen to skip a generation, maybe your children should leave less to their own children from their estate.

Also, be careful of your pride. Wanting your children and grandchildren to look a certain way could cause you to overindulge them with material things.

Finally, maximize the time you have left to counsel your children and grandchildren on what it means to be truly successful. A gray head is a wise head, as Proverbs says, and no greater input can be left to your family's future generations than how to wisely earn and steward money.

⁓ For Further Reflection ⁓

1. Can you recall a situation where cash from grandparents created a sticky situation for you or someone you know? How was the situation handled?

2. If you are a grandparent, have you discussed your estate and your giving plan with your children? Why or why not? Do you think you should?

3. Financial issues are difficult to discuss in many families. What can you do to open the communication lines in your family?

4. Have the thoughts in this chapter caused you to reconsider your estate plan? In what way?

A Second Chance

As Jim Conwell lay motionless on his hospital bed that morning, his mind was in a whirl. It was difficult to assimilate all that had happened during the past seventy-two hours. Being at church…Pastor Firnbeck's words about suffering loss…the ambulance…Jimmy's comments…the vivid recollection of the asset pile that grew and grew and was then gone. The successful surgery and the realization that he now had a second chance.

Although there was a lot to think about, Jim could see things more clearly now. God had let him stare death in the face to give him another chance to add some silver and gold to the pile. It was obvious to him now that his children, Jimmy and Jill, and all those folks from the church were the "precious stones" that would last into eternity and not be burned up.

How could I have been so shortsighted? he thought. *Why have I spent so much time working and ignoring my children? It wasn't intentional. It just sort of happened. Why don't I really care about other people in my life? Why are houses, cars, and country clubs so important to me? Why haven't I spent more time involved with godly endeavors?* As Jim pondered these issues, tears of repentance mingled with tears of joy as he acknowledged his gratefulness to God for giving him a second chance.

It shouldn't take a brush with death to help us see that the almost insatiable consumption mentality of the past has waned. Even the secular world acknowledges this trend as the present generation is facing harder times financially. Shouldn't we, as Christians, be at the forefront of this new thinking? Shouldn't we make the hard decisions regarding our money and our families so we can focus on what lasts into eternity? Isn't it time we became truly prosperous by focusing on leaving a godly posterity?

Jim got a second chance; we may not. After our works are tested by fire, will precious stones, gold, and silver remain (1 Corinthians 3:12)? That will be possible only if we live our lives wisely by focusing on the things that will last forever (our godly posterity) rather than the things that will burn (financial capital), and only if we earn and use our money with a focus on the eternal rather than the temporal.

May we build a legacy that will stand the test of fire!

Institute of Capital Development

- Music/Art
- Science
- Social Studies/History
- Mathematics
- English/Language/ Spelling/ Speaking
- Writing
- Reading
- Physical Education
- Foreign Language
- Technology

INTELLECTUAL/PHYSICAL

- Nutrition/Eating Habits
- Appearance
- Manners
- Financial/Budgeting (Stewardship)
- Work Ethic

- Accepting
- Authority
- Balance
- Bold
- Character
- Compassion
- Courage
- Courteous

- Determination
- Diligence
- Discipline
- Encouraging
- Endurance
- Generosity
- Honesty/Truthful
- Integrity

- Leadership
- Perseverance
- Poise
- Purpose
- Respectful
- Responsibility
- Self-control
- Significance
- Teachability

SOCIAL/EMOTIONAL

BASICS

- Being sure you are a Christian
- Spirit-filled life – loving, kind, patient, forgiving, giving, humble, obedient
- Attributes of God
- Studying the Bible
- Prayer
- Fellowship
- Witnessing

DEVELOPING CONVICTIONS

- Relationship/Friends
- Speech
- Dating
- Music/Movies
- Work
- Money
- Healthy Lifestyle

SPIRITUAL

Social Capital Goals

Accepting: To willingly or gladly accept others who are different from us without being judgmental; to see them as God sees them.

> *Measurement:* When we are able to have contact with others and not feel we are superior in any way because they might not measure up to the standards we expect of ourselves and because we know God made them and He has a purpose and a plan for everyone.

Authority: The power or right to command or act. This is the ability to exercise dominion and control.

> *Measurement:* A person understands authority when he or she exhibits submission to and follows the one who is in power.
>
> Note: Regardless of a person's position in life, there is always an authority over him or her. The ultimate authority is God, but in every relational setup, whether it be parent/child, boss/employee, CEO/board, there is always someone in authority over the people involved. Therefore, it is important to learn to submit to and acknowledge authority.

Balance: An influence or force tending to produce a stable or unchanging system.

> *Measurement:* Not becoming excessive in any area of life.

Bold: Fearless or courageous.

> *Measurement:* Being able to take a stand for God and His Word when necessary.

Character: Character is a distinctive quality assigned to a person by reputation or distinctive qualities of any kind and can be positive or negative. Character is what a person is and how he or she acts when no one else is around or watching.

> *Measurement:* Doing the right thing even when no one is around or watching.

Compassion: Showing empathy and being tenderhearted.

> *Measurement:* Exhibiting empathy and caring when someone else is hurting. Understanding how someone else is feeling as evidenced by kind words and a helping hand.

Courage: This is a quality of mind that enables a person to encounter danger and difficulties with firmness and without fear. It is also referred to as bravery, valor, and boldness—setting one's mind and being resolute to press on in the face of adversity.

> *Measurement:* Demonstrates the ability to overcome difficult situations and fears.

Courteous: Considerate toward others.

> *Measurement:* When thinking of others' needs first comes more naturally than thinking of yourself or your needs.

Determination: Firmness of purpose and resoluteness.

> *Measurement:* Keep going with our eyes on God even when faced with troubles or roadblocks.

Diligence: Firmly and constantly continuing onward with an assignment or project despite obstacles; attentive and energetic application to a task.

> *Measurement:* Characterized by a commitment to completing assignments on time, with concern for quality and appearance.

Discipline: The governance of one's conduct or practice. It is training for the purpose of becoming accustomed to order and subordination, and to act in accordance with rules. It is learning what you should and should not do.

> *Measurement:* Exhibits the qualities of stick-to-itiveness, restraint, and control in every endeavor undertaken.

Encourage: To give confidence or support to another.

> *Measurement:* Characterized by kind words or deeds done without being prompted by another.

Endurance: A state of lasting or duration without giving up, even in the midst of suffering, pain, or distress.

> *Measurement:* Persevering to the end of a goal by working through whatever is necessary to achieve it.

Generous: Liberal in giving, abundant, ample.

> *Measurement:* Sharing what we have with others in a kind manner.

Honest/Truthful: Fairness in dealing with others, free from fraud or theft. Reputable, suitable, and sincere.

> *Measurement:* Always truthful in everything that is said, and not tricky or deceitful.

Integrity: Behavior in accordance with a strict code of values—honesty and the quality of wholeness.

> *Measurement:* Always consistent in speech and behavior, of utmost character, and always saying what you mean and meaning what you say.

Leadership: Offering guidance by the hand, to guide or conduct by showing the way, to direct, to show the method of obtaining an objective. This involves helping others grow and perform.

> *Measurement:* Exhibit the ability to show others how to do something by setting the example and pointing the way. Seeing to it that someone else grows and succeeds.

Perseverance: Persistence in anything undertaken—to pursue steadily and not give up or abandon.

> *Measurement:* Seeing something through to the end, completing the task.

Poise: To be balanced; to maintain a state of equilibrium.

> *Measurement:* Not easily frustrated or knocked off center.

Respectful: To feel or show esteem or consideration for someone.

> *Measurement:* Characterized by treating others better than we care for ourselves.

Self-Control: Keeping one's emotions, desires, or actions in check by one's own will.

> *Measurement:* Characterized by keeping our emotions on an even keel.

Significance: Importance.

> *Measurement:* Understanding one's own view and value to God.

Teachability: A willingness to listen to new ideas and learn from others.

> *Measurement:* The willingness to listen sincerely to new ideas with discernment.

Notes

Chapter 1: A Glimpse of Eternity

1. This hypothetical story was written by Pat Harley to communicate Russ Crosson's key points.
2. Bill Richards, "Dear Mother Teresa, How Are You Fixed for Cash Just Now?" *Wall Street Journal.*
3. Randy Alcorn, *Money, Possessions, and Eternity* (Wheaton, IL: Tyndale, 1989), 59.

Chapter 2: Prosperity

1. Rosalie J. Slater, *American Dictionary of the English Language* (San Francisco: Foundation for American Christian Education, 1967), 9-11. It's also interesting that Noah Webster's dictionary flowed from his desire to establish for the infant country of America a common language consistent with its constitutional course. He knew that political separation from the Old World would not be enough to sustain this young republic if it did not also separate itself philosophically and educationally. Thus, a language was necessary for America that would avoid the corruption, folly, tyranny, and vices of Europe. Webster believed it should also promote virtue and patriotism and embellish and improve the sciences.
2. Paul Lee Tan, *Encyclopedia of 7700 Illustrations* (Rockville, MD: Assurance Publishers, 1979), 802.
3. Matthew Henry, *Commentary on the Whole Bible* (Grand Rapids, MI: Zondervan, 1961), 794-95.
4. Dennis Haack, "Which Success Really Counts?" *Moody Monthly,* March 1990.
5. Tan, *Encyclopedia of 7700 Illustrations,* 1374.
6. Haack, "Which Success Really Counts?"
7. Rob Phillips, "Beyond Success," *Sky,* November 1992, 18-22.

Chapter 3: Posterity

1. Additional verses on posterity include Psalm 103:17-18; 34:16; Exodus 20:5-6; Deuteronomy 7:9; Isaiah 59:21; 66:22.

Chapter 4: The Life-overview Balance Sheet

1. William R. Mattox, Jr., "The Family-Friendly Corporation, Strengthening the Ties that Bind," *Family Policy,* November 1992, 3.
2. Tan, *Encyclopedia of 7700 Illustrations,* 802.

Chapter 5: The Principle of Time Replacement

1. Charles R. Swindoll, *Living on the Ragged Edge* (Waco, TX: Word, 1985), 68.
2. Leon A. Danco, *Beyond Survival* (Reston, VA: Reston Publishing, 1975), 178.

3. "Graphics for Economic News Releases," Bureau of Labor Statistics, https://www.bls.gov/american-time-use/work-by-ftpt-job-edu-h.htm.

4. Richard A. Swenson, M.D., *Margin* (Colorado Springs: NavPress, 1992), 116.

5. Ibid., 15, 30.

6. Gil Schwartz, "Making the Case for Taking a Break," *Fortune,* 9 March 1992, 155.

7. Jeremy Rifkin, *Time Wars* (New York: Simon and Schuster, 1987), 59.

8. James Dobson, *Focus on the Family* newsletter, December 1992, 1-2.

9. Dr. Patrick T. Malone, "Heavy Stress Drives Motorists to Take Hostility on the Road," *Atlanta Journal and Constitution.*

10. Swenson, *Margin,* 88.

11. Essay from Life Messengers, 1926 Densmore Ave. N., Seattle, Washington 98133. Used by permission.

12. E.F. Schumacher, *Good Work* (New York: Simon and Schuster, 1987), 25.

13. Jeff Davidson, "A Father's Blessing," *Focus on the Family Magazine,* June 1986.

Chapter 6: A New Understanding of Work

1. Billy Graham, quoted in *Atlanta Journal and Constitution,* 17 August 1992.

2. Jane Fonda, quoted in *World Magazine,* 23 May 1992.

3. Pete Petit, quoted in *Delta In-Flight Magazine.*

4. Jim Henderson, "Lynch Quits While He's at the Top," *USA Today,* 29 March 1990.

5. Marjie McGraw, "A new world according to Garth," *First* magazine, 28 June 1993, 31.

6. Dan Stamp, quoted by Mark Stevens in "Workaholics Should Find Time to Enjoy Life," *Atlanta Journal and Constitution,* 15 May 1989.

7. Jeffrey A. Tannenbaum, "Entrepreneurs and Second Acts," *Wall Street Journal.*

8. William Johnston, quoted by Susan Dentzer in "How We Will Live," *U.S. News & World Report,* 25 December 1989.

9. Mattox, *Family Policy.*

10. Lesley Alderman, *Money,* December 1991, 75.

11. C.H. Spurgeon, *The Treasury of David* (McLean, VA: MacDonald, nd), 88.

12. Phillips, "Beyond Success," 22.

13. Ibid.

Chapter 7: Wanting It All

1. Carrie Teegardin, "Load Too Heavy for Many," *Atlanta Journal and Constitution,* 6 September 1992.

2. Ibid.

3. Dr. James C. Dobson, *Focus on the Family* newsletter, February 1994.

4. Letter to Ronald Blue and Company, 19 July 1991. Used by permission.

Chapter 8: Train Up a Child

1. J.K. Gresset, quoted by Patrick Morley in *The Man in the Mirror* (Nashville: Thomas Nelson, 1992), 235.

2. A.W. Tozer, quoted by Dr. Charles R. Swindoll, *For Those Who Hurt* (Grand Rapids, MI: Zondervan, 1994).

3. Alcorn, *Money, Possessions and Eternity,* 373.

4. R.C. Sproul, "The Problems of Pain and Pleasure," *Table Talk,* July 1992.

5. J.I. Packer, *Knowing God* (Downers Grove, IL: InterVarsity, 1973), 18-19.

Chapter 9: A Good Name Is Better Than Riches

1. Alcorn, *Money, Possessions and Eternity,* 374.

2. Chuck Colson, "Not Even a Christian Echo," *World,* 3 October 1992.

Chapter 10—An Alternative Investment, Part 1

1. See at www.ageoflearning.com/readingstudy/November 15, 2018.

Chapter 11—An Alternative Investment, Part 2

1. Dorothy Patterson, "The High Calling of Wife and Mother in Biblical Perspective," in *Recovering Biblical Manhood and Womanhood*, eds. John Piper and Wayne Grudem (Wheaton, IL: Crossway, 1991), 366-367.

Chapter 12—Contentment: Productive vs. Consumptive

1. Randall Poe, "The SOB's," *Across the Board*, May 1980, 27.

2. Patrick Reynolds, *The Gilded Leaf* (Backinprint.com, 2006), 2.

3. Reynolds, *The Gilded Leaf.*

Other Great Reading by Russ Crosson

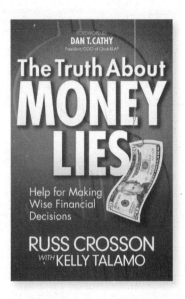

The Truth About Money Lies

Russ teams up with gifted communicator Kelly Talamo to debunk popular money lies that influence your spending decisions. Through personal stories and relevant examples, the authors expose the underlying assumptions in the world's beliefs and then give principles based on God's Word to provide the truth and give sound advice. Some of the lies covered are:

- Taxes are my biggest problem.
- I can't afford to give.
- My security is in my investments.
- My talents and abilities produce my wealth.
- The harder I work, the more money I make.

After reading *The Truth About Money Lies,* you'll be better equipped to make wise budget decisions, spend money responsibly, and manage finances.

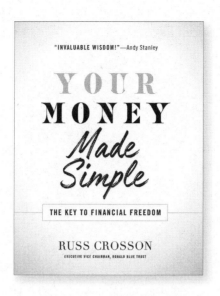

Your Money Made Simple

Does successfully making the most of your money feel like a mystery? Are you wondering where it goes or how to get a grip on your spending?

Author and Christian financial advisor Russ Crosson has spent more than 40 years guiding individuals and couples in everyday financial situations. In *Your Money Made Simple*, he offers the key to mastering your finances biblically—and it's not about how much money you make.

Customized to meet your needs, this resource teaches you how to manage your income wisely by...

- Offering proven formulas that work for any income level, age, or vocation.
- Setting you on a path to freedom from financial worries.
- Including easy-to-use financial planning tools and graphic charts.

Packed with wisdom and practical applications, this book will help you make the most of your money and how you spend it.

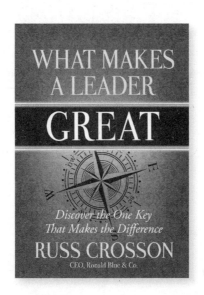

What Makes a Leader Great

What makes a good leader? Russ Crosson knows—and he learned the hard way: "It's doubtful that anyone can lead effectively until they've been humbled or hurt deeply."

The result of Russ's humbling experience has taught him that leadership success isn't about the leader at all. It's about the mission of the organization, church, business, or even family where the leader serves. It's about who will replace you when you're gone.

If you're interested in the true bottom line on leadership success, here is a concise but on-target look at what true leadership is like. Russ emphasizes the need for leaders to think about the legacy of their leadership.

There are many books that are "leadership how-tos" or "what to do" books. Here is something different: a **why**-to book that will help you succeed in more important ways than you ever imagined.

RonaldBlueTrust®
Wisdom for Wealth. *For Life.*

CORPORATE PROFILE

With nationwide capabilities, Ronald Blue Trust provides wealth management strategies and trust services based on biblical principles to help clients make wise financial decisions, live generously, and leave a lasting legacy. Through a network of 14 branch offices, we serve clients in all 50 states through four distinct divisions and offer services across the wealth spectrum in these key areas:

- Financial, retirement, and estate planning
- Investment management and solutions
- Charitable giving strategies
- Personal trust and estate settlement services
- Bill paying services
- Family office services
- Business consulting services
- Institutional client services

Ronald Blue Trust offers many resources on the topics of financial planning, giving, family & life, economy & investments, leadership, and retirement. Some of the wisdom we offer on these subjects comes in the form of books which include the following titles: *Your Life…Well Spent, The Truth About Money Lies, What Makes a Leader Great, Your Money Made Simple,* and *Faces of Generosity.* Please visit www .ronblue.com to view newsletters and videos in our Library, subscribe to our Insights blog, and learn more about our services.

Ronald Blue Trust Branch Offices

Atlanta, GA	Holland, MI	Nashville, TN
Baltimore, MD	Houston, TX	Orange County, CA
Charlotte, NC	Indianapolis, IN	Orlando, FL
Chicago, IL	Montgomery, AL	Phoenix, AZ
Greenville, SC		Seattle, WA

Contacting Ronald Blue Trust

www.ronblue.com	800-841-0362	1125 Sanctuary Parkway
info@ronblue.com	Fax: 770-280-6001	Suite 500
		Alpharetta, GA 30009

To learn more about Harvest House books and
to read sample chapters, visit our website:

www.harvesthousepublishers.com

HARVEST HOUSE PUBLISHERS
EUGENE, OREGON